The Book of the
BR STANDARDS : 2

That Standard look: Willesden shed in 1963. Photograph J.G. Walmsley, The Transport Treasury.

A British Railways Illustrated Special

By Richard Derry

With Contributions From
Philip Atkins
Allan C. Baker
R.H.N. Hardy

Copyright IRWELL PRESS LIMITED
ISBN 1-903266-32-7
First published in the United Kingdom in 2002
by Irwell Press Limited, 59A, High Street, Clophill,
Bedfordshire MK45 4BE
Printed by Newton Printing

Dedication

For Chris Hawkins and George Reeve of the Irwell Press, from a grateful author.

73088 JOYOUS GARD at a shed 'somewhere on the Southern' in the early 1960s. An irresistible picture to remind us that all was not romance in the steam era. Nothing 'Joyous' about this job! Yet to work on the Standards was a much brighter prospect than say, a D49, a Lord Nelson, a Compound or anything Great Western. You oiled them from the outside and though it remained hard toil, there was none of the aching manhandling of Dark Ages ironmongery in dropping the fire and this particular job, clearing the smokebox (while still horrible) did not need to be done every day at least. Photograph J.G. Walmsley, The Transport Treasury.

A Note on Engine History Cards

Details are from the BR9215 Engine Record Cards held at the PRO, Kew and the BR ERO 3666 cards held at the National Railway Museum, York. Of the mileage figures that appear with the Shops entry, the first is entered under "Since previous General or Intermediate repair" and the second figure is entered under the heading "Jan 1st to date shopped".

The other mileage figure is part of the Annual statistics entry on the ERO 3666 cards; they are not complete, nor are the works visits or the boiler records. I assume the tender records are correct. Much is omitted from the cards, frustratingly; the BR Standards all inherited a type of record based on the LMS system which left out much important information such as cylinders and motion which were recorded separately. These all seem to have been lost, alas. Mileages were a joke to some shed staff, yet it was all assiduously gathered in and if the figures were inflated or conflated, then it was, at least, done in the same way for every engine. Interpretations were also different then. Take a look at CLAN BUCHANAN. It's 'date to traffic' was immediately followed, it would seem, by its weighing and painting... Hmmm. You have to suspect that this was a case of getting the annual production figures 'upped' just in time at the year end. Yet this is part of the attraction – search for your own 'compromises' in the official record! The overhaul classifications are thus:-

NC = Non Classified
LC = Light Casual
HC = Heavy Casual
LI = Light Intermediate
HI = Heavy Intermediate
HG = Heavy General
U = Unclassified
[EO] = Engine Order
G&C = Gresham and Craven

Cut up dates are from Peter Hands' 'What Happened to Steam' books; these are slightly different from the RCTS History which states that 72000-72004 were destroyed by 15 February 1964.

Readers of 'The Book Of' series (I hope a lot more BR Standard Engine Histories will appear in a further *Book of the BR Standards: 3*) will know of the delights and drawbacks of the BR Engine History Cards, which have been gone into many times. They are the best record we have (though they do 'tail off' markedly in the 1960s) but do not 'tie down' a locomotive to a day or hour as some have believed over the years. They represent the surviving traces of a vast paper trail in the days before computers when even telephones were a rarity. Days could be 'fudged' at the end or beginning of the month to suit targets and different works recorded different events in different ways. It is not always easy to reconcile all this. Yet, understood for what they are and without silly attempts to paint 'wrinkles' as shocking revelations they remain a treasure trove, the most complete body of data we have.

Contents

In a statement truly of the blindingly obvious, in The Book of the BR Standards it was declared 'It is not easy to illustrate 999 locomotives!' This remains true even with a second shot at it though we must be a fair way down the road now. Yet the old riddle of the quart and the pint pot, as lamented in the earlier book, remains as daunting as it always was. Unlike the first book, this is not an attempt to 'showcase' the Standards class by class and to tell their story. This is more a celebration of those 999 engines with some rather more 'in depth' approaches to some aspects of their construction and operation, from a trio of experts kindly arranged through the good offices of the publisher. All the Building Dates, Allocations, Tenders, Types, Lot Numbers and Names and all the rest (or a lot of them at least) were set down in the earlier book which, though long unavailable, has now been (or will soon be) put back into print.

Richard Derry, September 2002

The Britannia cab which had been mocked up so assiduously while the design was being worked out. The famous mock-up had been completed at Derby as far back as 1949 and taken down to London for inspection. Similar concoctions were made at Brighton for the 2-6-4T and at Swindon for the Class 3 2-6-2T. Photograph The Transport Treasury.

Britannias in the Age of Elizabeth

Getting There and Beyond

By Philip Atkins

The first British Railways Standard locomotive, 4-6-2 No.70000 BRITANNIA, entered service in January 1951, just three years after nationalisation, and also fifty years to the month since the death of Queen Victoria, on the eve of the second Elizabethan Age. A close contemporary in the transportation field was the tragically flawed de Havilland Comet I jet airliner. Whereas the Comet was the end of the beginning, of the extraordinarily rapid development of jet propulsion, BRITANNIA was the beginning of the end. By 1970 men had landed on the Moon, but the steam locomotive was already extinct on British Railways.

The BR Standards in general could trace their descent directly back to the epoch-making prototype Churchward Great Western Railway taper boiler 4-6-0 No.98, which was completed at Swindon Works towards the end of 1903. It is intriguing to consider that a leading figure in its design, Oscar Deverell, had only entered the Drawing Office five years before, and that when he had commenced employment as a turner in 1888 the Works was building the last new (albeit very short-lived) broad gauge engines! No.98 was heavily influenced by contemporary American locomotive practice, particularly the inwardly inclined steam chests, and internal Stephenson valve gear. Ironically these features would very soon become superseded in US designs, but would be faithfully replicated in new locomotives, particularly 4-6-0s, built at Swindon until as late as 1950, by which time the BR Standards were already on the drawing board.

The tapered Belpaire boiler was also based on current Brooks Locomotive Works practice, although generally speaking Belpaire boilers were rare in the USA, with the notable exception of the Pennsylvania Railroad.

It was a lone 4-6-2 on the PRR, which strangely actually had a *round-topped* boiler, No.7067 delivered by the Pittsburgh Locomotive Works in 1907, which was the unwitting forerunner of BRITANNIA and countless other main line steam locomotives which would be built for service in nearly every part of the world over the next *eighty* years. It could validly lay claim to be the first *modern* steam locomotive, having outside cylinders with external Walschaerts valve gear, backed up by a generously large boiler with wide firebox. It possessed a curiously attractive austere charm, and but for the rapid adoption of the smoketube superheater soon afterwards from c.1910 it could be argued that except in sheer size the steam locomotive did not otherwise *significantly* progress from that point.

Almost identical 4-6-2s were also delivered to the rival (as far as the New York-Chicago passenger services were concerned) New York Central Railroad, which through successive classes of 'Pacific' until 1925, were thence progressively developed through several *marques* of 4-6-4, to culminate in the magnificent 'Niagara' 4-8-4 of 1945. Similar characteristics could be discerned in the 3ft 6in South African '25' and 5ft gauge Russian 'P36', both likewise 4-8-4s, built in the 1950s. In India were the numerous metre and 5ft 6in gauge 4-6-2s and 2-8-2s which continued to be built throughout the 1960s. In China there were the ponderous 'QJ' 2-10-2s constructed until the late 1980s, and also the attractive little 'SY' 2-8-2s built for industry even into the 1990s.

Although the Edwardian era, deemed by convention to have continued until 1914, is closely associated with elegant but user *un*friendly inside cylinder locomotives,

The first steaming of 70000, not yet named, at Crewe on 2 January 1951. One of its first real jobs after naming on 30 January was, appropriately, 'The Norfolkman' out of Liverpool Street on 1 February. A year later, on 11 February 1952 BRITANNIA had charge of the Royal Funeral Train from Wolferton to Kings Cross, in dismal rain.

The Rt Hon Alfred Barnes, long-forgotten Minister of Transport, performed the naming ceremony for BRITANNIA, at Marylebone on 30 January 1950. Here is the intrepid Minister at the controls of 70000, 'which he drove a short way out of the station and back'.

by the time it ended the first stirrings of utility were becoming unmistakably apparent. External Walschaerts valve gear was fitted to the generally forgotten first Gresley Great Northern Railway 2-6-0 No.1640 in 1912, and on the first Urie London & South Western Railway 4-6-0 No.486 in 1913. It would have similarly featured on the first Maunsell South Eastern & Chatham Railway 2-6-0 No.810, probably in 1915, whose *debut* was delayed by some two years by the exigencies of World War 1. Towards the end of the latter conflict, in late 1917, the Association of Railway Locomotive Engineers (ARLE) which for many years in peacetime had leisurely sought to harmonise fine details of locomotive design (e.g. tyre profiles) between companies, radically proposed that a series of national standard locomotive designs be prepared for construction after peace had been restored. These would conform to a new national loading gauge, the impetus for which would be the construction of the often mooted Channel Tunnel.

This dream only began to approach reality thirty years later with the nationalisation of Britain's by then 'grouped' railways (1923) in 1948. Just as the ARLE Standards would have been, the new British Railways Standards were overseen by a committee. Commencing in March 1949 this met every four weeks (strictly *not* monthly) and was comprised of the regional chief locomotive draughtsmen, under the enthusiastic chairmanship of E.S. Cox, late of the LMS. He summarised his initial proposals, which were not fully endorsed, in a report dated June 1948. This august body would solemnly debate such diverse topics in a single meeting as the quality of corks for oiling holes in coupling rods, to whether or not to adopt a double as opposed to a single exhaust in the new 4-6-2s. The 2-8-2 *versus* 2-10-0 question in 1951 was an executive decision taken by R.A. Riddles. It was perhaps inevitable that the ideas of what had been by far the largest constituent of BR, the former LMS, should predominate (just as in France likewise the philosophy of the old PLM was clearly apparent in some of the SNCF standard locomotive designs). However, many of the LMS features could, via William Stanier's 1932 move, be traced directly back to the GWR, while a few features espoused by the former LNER and Southern were also worked in for good measure.

Several of the new classes were in reality little more than cosmetic re-vamps of existing pre-1948 LMS standard classes, but the BR Standards nevertheless managed to project a strong measure of distinctive homogeneity. This could largely be ascribed to the highly talented Derby draughtsman, F.G. Carrier. The 'trademark' of the Standards was the bold slanted front of the running board, directly ahead of the cylinders, whose inclination of 67 degrees, determined as a result of wind tunnel tests, was ratified by the Committee in May 1950. Even E.S. Cox never stated where this particular feature came from. It was reminiscent of the styling of the attractive Chapelon 141P 2-8-2s on the SNCF, but much nearer home it could also have been a throwback to an abortive LMS 1931 proposal to modernise the ex-LNW 'Prince of Wales' 4-6-0s.

An inspired psychological move was to give different drawing offices overall responsibility for different classes, and

GEOFFREY CHAUCER looks suitably gorgeous as waning sunlight finds its way down through the murk to the Liverpool Street turntable, on 18 July 1958. Photograph The Transport Treasury.

also for certain specific components across the entire range. Thus Doncaster was allotted the Class 4 2-6-0 and the Class 5 4-6-0. The latter had not featured in Cox's initial June 1948 scheme, and curiously Doncaster Works had got by for half a century without designing or building a 4-6-0. Doncaster also had responsibility for designing coupling rods, which were originally intended to be of 'I' section, but which soon had to be redesigned in plain section, following problems with buckled rods on the early 4-6-2s. Indeed, even after a new design was

70004 WILLIAM SHAKESPEARE arrayed for the Golden Arrow, on the front of the shed at Stewarts Lane, 15 September 1957. It is well cleaned but that's only half the work now that polishing brightwork, motions, buffers, steelwork and the cab interior is a thing of the past – see Richard Hardy's 'Specialised Work'. The nameplate is now painted black and the hollow axles are gone but very few changes have been made to the design in its six years. Photograph R.C. Riley, The Transport Treasury.

700009 ALFRED THE GREAT runs into Norwich Thorpe with 'The Broadsman' on 15 August 1953. A platform end oik, in his short trousers and long socks, is pushing his luck at the very end of the platform. Photograph R.C. Riley, The Transport Treasury.

70014 IRON DUKE on the Arrow at Victoria Platform 8, its regular starting point. A wet and gloomy day in February 1957 and Syd Norman, Shop Officeman, has put the many times washed flags on the buffer beam. The Stewarts Lane long lamp irons are still in place despite a visit to Crewe Works. The train is shorter and in that summer three ordinary coaches were added to the head going down. The disc code is interesting: everybody knew the Golden Arrow would normally go down the main to Tonbridge but the code is Nunhead and Bexley Heath, a practice that started with headlamps going out on the buffer beam in the up journey back in 1952-53. See 'Specialised Work'. Photograph R.C. Riley, The Transport Treasury.

70016 ARIEL, in a state to shame a WD or a 9F, at Chester with a Holyhead-Birmingham train, July 1963. Photograph The Transport Treasury.

put into traffic there were numerous problems to be solved, sometimes with considerable urgency, as with 'Britannias' following their inauspicious *debut* in East Anglia in 1951, and with the first '9F' 2-10-0s in South Wales in 1954. Reference was made earlier to the Comet I airliner, which was at the very 'cutting edge' of contemporary technology and which sadly resulted in some 100 fatalities. After 120 years by the 1950s the steam locomotive was hardly 'cutting edge', but as the legendary S.O. Ell at Swindon neatly summed up it was (still) 'loved by all but understood by none'. Thus seemingly very minor design features, such as handrails on the smoke deflectors and slide bar fixings were respectively directly responsible for serious fatal derailments involving 'Britannias' near Didcot in 1955 and near Settle in 1960. For good measure, over a period of several years these engines also displayed a disconcerting tendency to part company from their tenders at speed, quite remarkably without any serious consequences. Cylinder lubrication was never fully mastered and there were problems with the balancing on the Class 3 2-6-2Ts.

Cox made regular visits to the regional design offices at Brighton, Derby, Doncaster and Swindon to discuss problems 'on the ground'. In January 1954 he inspected the newly completed Class 3 2-6-0 No.77000 at Swindon and was not overly impressed by its aesthetics. Contrary to the attractive original 1949 scheme (see the diagram in 'Standards That Never Were' later in this book) with its low running board as per its 2-6-2T equivalent, as actually designed and built the format followed that of the larger-boilered Class 4 2-6-0 on which the high running board did not look particularly amiss. Instructions were given to see what might be done to improve appearances, but in all probability the parts had already been made for the pilot twenty engines, and in the event no more were built and no alterations made.

The 'Britannia' 4-6-2s bore a close resemblance to the New South Wales C38 4-6-2s, which quite definitely had been inspired by the Pennsylvania K4 'Pacifics' of 1914. Drawings for the latter were extensively published in *Engineering* during 1917, and the excellent proportions of the boiler reputedly provided the basis for that on the first Gresley 4-6-2 built in 1922. This proved to be remarkably enduring and is traceable through to the final Peppercorn 'A1' built in 1949. The round-topped firebox apart the general external dimensions closely anticipated those of the BR Class 7, which also incorporated the Doncaster style three-bar slide bar assembly which had actually been pioneered on a PRR 4-4-0 in 1894. Incidentally, like the Pennsylvania K4 the 'Britannia' changed from fluted to plain side rods, and was paired with a variety of different tenders.

Even the evolution of the BR 9 2-10-0 from the BR 7 4-6-2 merely repeated what had happened on the Pennsylvania Railroad nearly forty years earlier. The PRR designed the K4 passenger 4-6-2 and an interchangeable freight 2-8-2, the L1, in tandem at Altoona. In 1948 Cox had envisaged the standard BR heavy freight engine similarly as being a 2-8-2 interchangeable with the mixed traffic 4-6-2. In the event, in 1951, it was decided to opt for 2-10-0 instead. Again the PRR had already been there, having similarly evolved a 2-10-0 (the I1s) in 1916, and several hundred each of the L1 and I1s were built. The K4 was also stretched into the M1 4-8-2 in 1923, which had no BR 'equivalent', and also inflated it into the K5 'super Pacific', of which only two appeared in 1929. One of these was initially fitted with Caprotti valve gear (shades of BR

71000), but in all these five classes, which totalled precisely 1,900 engines, grate area was a uniform 70 sq ft, *originally hand fired* in the case of the 4-6-2s and 2-8-2s as built!

Scrapping of each of these classes commenced in the late 1940s before the first BR Standard had even materialised, and continued apace during the early 1950s while these were appearing on the scene. Even here there were curious parallels for the once self-styled 'Standard Railroad of the World' was anything but standard when it came to increasingly frantic diesel procurement between 1946 and 1956. The standard PRR steam classes were vanquished by a whole variety of diesels in much the same manner as would be the BR Standards in the 1960s.

There were even certain affinities between Altoona and Crewe, where standard locomotives were nothing new, long before 1948 or even 1932. Under John Ramsbottom in the 1860s Crewe had built nearly as many engines of a single class, the 'DX' 0-6-0, as the grand total of all the BR Standards put together nearly a century later. Locomotive standardisation was practised to a greater or lesser extent by several major British railway companies, particularly as regards boilers and boiler components. Contrary to popular belief it was not 'invented' by G.J. Churchward on the GWR around 1903.

However, British excursions in this field paled by comparison with those abroad, particularly in Germany and Russia. On the Prussian State Railway (KPEV) most locomotive classes numbered at least several hundred engines, and some several thousand. Most prolific was the G8 0-8-0 which totalled very nearly 5,000 units, but even this hardly compared with the Russian 'E' 0-10-0, built between 1912 and 1957, which although admittedly comprised of several *marques,* at a conservative estimate ultimately embraced 11,000 engines.

In 1925 the German State Railway (DR) embarked on an ambitious locomotive standardisation programme. This was inaugurated by an entirely new two-cylinder 4-6-2 symbolically numbered 01.001, and some 2,250 standard locomotives of various classes were built under *normal* circumstances up to 1939, which latterly included 4-6-4, 4-8-4, and 2-10-2 designs not envisaged a decade earlier.

Germany ranked second as a steam locomotive builder only to the United States, where ordinarily locomotive standardisation was anathema. However, following the placing of the American railroads under government control the newly formed United States Railroad Administration in 1918 instituted a wide range of standard locomotives which ranged from 0-6-0 to 2-8-8-2, which proved highly successful in the pre-'Super Power' era. Even after the last US 4-6-4, 2-8-4 and 4-8-4 locomotives were built commercially in 1948-49 the Norfolk & Western Railway was constructing new 0-8-0s and (compound) 2-8-8-2s, which were directly descended from the USRA designs, in its own Roanoke Shops as late as 1952-53.

Steam locomotive construction on a large scale during the 1960s was confined to India, and thereafter, although this was not initially generally realised, to China where it actually expanded rapidly during the 1970s. Post-war steam locomotive deliveries to the Indian railways were dominated by two wheel arrangements, 4-6-2 and 2-8-2, for both the broad (5ft 6in) and metre gauges. As in Germany and on BR the *doyen* was a two-cylinder 4-6-2, No.7200. Delivered by the Baldwin Locomotive Works in 1947, it set the basic pattern for no fewer than 5,281 engines of five classes built until 1972. Almost all of these were still in service in mid-1981, when they accounted for over 70 per cent of the by-then declining Indian steam locomotive stock.

Even greater dominance was later achieved in China by only *two* locomotive classes, the JS 2-8-2 and QJ 2-10-2, both introduced in 1956-57. Both, likewise, remained in production until 1988, by which time the combined total was about 6,600. (Curiously,

70018 FLYING DUTCHMAN, viewed from the platform at Temple Meads, with Bath Road shed in the background, 8 August 1954. Construction of the Britannias was by now drawing to a close; as FLYING DUTCHMAN made for this stirring sight, 70052 was being painted at Crewe while 70053 and 70054 were nearly complete in the Erecting Shop.

respective sub-totals in 1988 were already significantly below the known class totals, despite an avowed 'economic life' of 45 years). Whereas in 1978 these two classes together accounted for only 49 per cent of the total Chinese steam locomotive stock, then at its all time peak of around 7,800, by 1988 this had risen to no less than 87 per cent. In 1992 this proportion had further increased to 96 per cent, but by then the steam fleet was already in precipitate decline despite the fact that some 2,000 2-8-2s and 2-10-2s had been built at Datong *after* 1980! By comparison developments in China in the 1990s have put the premature demise of the British Railways Standards in the 1960s completely in the shade!

Canton's 70026 POLAR STAR with The Red Dragon waiting to depart Cardiff on 2 June 1953 – extra Coronation crown on the train headboard. Photograph R.C. Riley, The Transport Treasury.

70030 WILLIAM WORDSWORTH comes past Ipswich shed with a London train. Another Britannia stands on one of the shed roads behind the diesel shunter. It was the coming of further Britannias at the end of 1952 and in 1953 (70035-70042) together with others such as 70030 off the LMR that enabled engine workings and train services on the Liverpool Street to Cambridge and Norwich route to be reorganised to match the Liverpool Street to Norwich via Ipswich services, already famously accelerated with the appearance of the first Britannias. The gains were radical, ten minutes to Cambridge and twenty minutes to Norwich via Ely. Some WR expresses, to the West of England and South Wales, were accelerated at the same time; the publicity, tellingly, made no mention of BR Pacifics...

70034 THOMAS HARDY, one of the 'second wave' of GE stalwarts, at Willesden during its allocation there from March 1963. In June the following year it went to Crewe North. Photograph J.G. Walmsley, The Transport Treasury.

Left. 70039 SIR CHRISTOPHER WREN, by now with the post-Milton 'Scot type' handholds on the smoke deflectors, stands on the engine siding at Liverpool Street, 31 January 1959. Time was already being called on the GE Britannias. The slogan 'Come Back To The Sun At Clacton' had appeared only the year before, with Britannias put on the 'Essex Coast Express' for business traffic but by June 1959 the Clacton interval service was in the hands of Brush Type 2s. The 'Essex Coast Express' remained Britannia hauled but it would not last long. The concentration of Britannias at Norwich, subsequent storage at March and their sending elsewhere was not far off. Photograph The Transport Treasury.

Below. 70040 CLIVE OF INDIA runs into Kings Cross with one of the Grimsby trains. This was one of the first three, 70039-70041, to be released from storage at March at the end of 1960. Going to Immingham, they presented B1 crews on the onerous London jobs with undreamed of power and they revelled in the work, much as the GE Stratford and Norwich men had done nearly a decade before. Four more came in 1961 adding to the already wonderful Pacific mix on the GN in the south but with the end of steam in 1963 the Britannias were on the move again. Photograph The Transport Treasury.

70042 makes for a fine portrait at Liverpool Street, 11 May 1957. Photograph R.C. Riley, The Transport Treasury.

The sleek and 'means business' look of the Britannia, a quality enhanced by the big 1D tenders attached to the last ten. 70053 MORAY FIRTH is at Willesden, 28 July 1963.

The stirring air of the Britannia names faltered at odd junctures. There was the dull civil servant Lord Hurcomb (no personal slight intended but Hotspur he weren't), the curiously anonymous 70047 and THE TERRITORIAL ARMY 1908-1958. The TA of course could not be more deserving of a locomotive name but it sat oddly with the likes of VULCAN and ROBIN HOOD. Mind you, 70048 was at one time to have been called FURNESS so perhaps we should be grateful.

'The Duke'

'The Duke' at Camden, 20 May 1958. The big tender with its ten ton capacity was the second of two that were unique. The first had been the 1E – basically a 1D but with ten tons nominal capacity rather than nine. It was the first of the BR tenders to have a coal pusher, as in LM Stanier Pacific practice. It was replaced by the specially built 1J, with rather more coal and less water, towards the end of 1957 (actual date recorded was 9 November). It is recognisable by having far less of a 'cutaway' at the rear. The type 13 boiler was similar to the Britannia but the firebox was a foot longer. Had the British Caprotti gear with the final cam box design seen on 71000, 44686 and 44687 and 73125-73154 come say, ten years earlier, there is little doubt that it would have been applied more or less universally on BR. Photograph J. Robertson, The Transport Treasury.

71000 (together with 92014 en route to the Willesden Exhibition, passing Bushey on 18 May 1954. DUKE OF GLOUCESTER was named to mark the Duke's honorary Presidency of the International Railway Congress in London, which was celebrated in the Willesden Exhibition. Photograph H.C. Casserley.

Yet more inspection, this time at Crewe Paint Shop, May 1954. Photograph A.G. Ellis, The Transport Treasury.

'The Duke' passing Camden shed with a down parcels train on 31 August 1961. Its stamping ground was really Crewe-London and it became closely associated with the Mid-Day Scot but was never popular, with crews convinced that it deteriorated as the working week progressed. By Friday you couldn't do anything with it! Photograph Peter Groom.

Gathering of The Clans

On 16 June 1956 a gathering of the Clan Cameron was held at Achnacarry Castle near Spean Bridge and BR rose to the occasion by turning out the appropriately named 72001. This was the only time, apart from one or two trial runs, that the class ventured into these wild and desolate parts. The train here is awaiting a crossing at Tyndrum Upper. Photograph J.L. Stevenson, courtesy Hamish Stevenson.

A twilit Clan. 72007 stripped of plates and with 12A simply painted on the smokebox door, fulminates at Kingmoor on 15 April 1965. Photograph The Transport Treasury.

72006 at Carlisle Citadel on 5 September 1961. The AWS battery box is a clear feature on the right-hand running plate and, 72001 aside doing its ancestral duty, the notorious 'flexible screen' is prominent on the Clans in these pictures. It was introduced on the earlier Britannias and the Clans with 'inset' tenders, as detailed by Allan Baker in the section 'Maintaining Standards'. Despite the work that went into maintaining the screens, and various efforts with different materials and fastenings, they never really lasted long. Photograph F.W. Smith, The Transport Treasury.

72000 CLAN BUCHANAN, 'flexible screen' flapping, at Haymarket shed in 1954. The Clans were always in danger of falling between two stools; there were after all plenty of good Class 5s available. Crews, moreover, might come in contact with one of these Pacifics only sporadically, or hardly at all and they wouldn't like anything out of the ordinary. The other stool was that, 'if it looks like a Pacific it must be worth something' and Class 7 duties when the Clans inevitably found themselves on them were a bit too much. And just how many jobs were tailored to Class 6 anyway? Not many. Cox's comment that the Clans were 'a border line case' had more meaning than he thought; after all, many were stationed at the 'The Border' – Carlisle – and all spent their time crossing it back and forth! Photograph The Transport Treasury.

'The Standard 5 is Good' wrote 'Mac' in a 1951 edition of the 'Scottish Region Magazine' - his headline for an account of a journey with 73009 on the 10am Glasgow Buchanan Street to Aberdeen that year. The first 'Standard 5', 73000, spent the 1950s at former Midland sheds though when recorded here at Bristol Barrow Road on 5 July 1959 its home shed of Grimesthorpe had recently passed to the Eastern Region. The first five '5's, 73000-73004 went to the Midland and 73005-73009, a couple of months after 73000's appearance, went to Scotland. Photograph R.C. Riley, The Transport Treasury.

'The Standard 5 is Good'

73005, the first of the Class 5s to go to Scotland. It went to Perth in June 1951 and stayed there until driven out by dieselisation in 1963. It finished up at Corkerhill. The BR Class 5s were in essence the LMS Black Five as developed by the 1940s; they had the LMS 3B sloping throatplate boiler with some adapted fittings but the two types were not precisely alike; there was several inches difference in lengths and the BR engines had 6ft 2in driving wheels while the Black Fives had 6ft drivers. The cylinders were different and of course the looks, with the cab and high running plate, were widely apart. Photograph W. Hermiston, The Transport Treasury.

73059 at Polmadie about 1955. Derby built the first hundred BR Class 5s under five separate Lots and shared the rest with Doncaster. Crewe, on the other hand, built most of the boilers for Derby (130 plus twelve spares); of the rest Doncaster built ten boilers for its own Class 5s while Darlington supplied it with thirty-four more. Compare the cab with, say 73000 and 73005; from the 1954 orders onwards the rear ends of the Standard cabs were altered in response to complaints of draughts. The earlier pattern was a handrail pillar running from the rear of the footplate upwards to the extension of the cab roof. From now on there would just be the simple handrail on the tender, as on 73059. Photograph J. Robertson, The Transport Treasury.

Top right. A BR Class 5 on the Western Region. 73039 runs past Aller Junction with a freight on 2 August 1955. In the main, the only Class 5s the Western Region got from new were actually Caprottis, but they spent only a year or two at Shrewsbury before moving *en-masse* to Patricroft. Other, 'normal', Class 5s found their way on to the Western from new (or nearly new), 73039 coming to St Phillip's Marsh in September 1953. Few in number and scattered, reaction to the engines on the WR was muted to say the least. Deficiencies such as the draughts, and driving on the 'wrong' side were amplified while the servicing advantages over the inside valve gear of the contemporary Halls and Granges and the rest were easily overlooked. Photograph J. Robertson, The Transport Treasury.

Below. 73109 at its home shed, Eastfield, when newish, about 1956-57; like other Standards, the Class 5s looked more purposeful with the high sided tenders – in this case the BR1B of 7 tons and 4,725 gallons capacity. The high running plates, so prominent on the Class 5s and other Standards, was carried on the boiler not the mainframe (apart from the sloping section) and various pipes were run neatly out of sight under it. There, it was thought, they would be free of vibration, differential expansion and so on. Photograph J. Robertson, The Transport Treasury.

Below right. One of the Southern's named engines, 73111 KING UTHER about 1963, probably at Nine Elms and suitably begrimed for the period. 73111 has the BR1F tender, with higher sides at the rear and a capacity of seven tons and 5,625 gallons. St Rollox was always notable for the large cabside numerals it applied to engines under its care but Doncaster (73111 was one of a number built there in 1955) it turns out, put larger numerals on all the Standards it built, except for the Class 4 2-6-0s. 73111 has smaller numerals here, later in its life, which presumably denotes a visit to Eastleigh in the meantime. Photograph J.G. Walmsley, The Transport Treasury.

73039
717
73039

73111
261
73111

73068 at an unknown date. It carries an 82E Bristol Barrow Road shed plate; it had gone there in May 1957 and did not leave till September 1962. The old Midland shed had passed to the Western Region with this 82 Bristol Division code in February 1958 so that gives us the spread of years of the picture. Absence of AWS (though not all Class 5s got it, by any means) and electrification flashes certainly makes it before about 1962. What is unusual is that 73068 is at New England shed; that, and its relatively bright condition would suggest a recent visit to Doncaster (where it *didn't* get the larger numerals – these only went on when built, it would seem). The usual generous interpretation of 'running-in' time would have ensued before its hand-over to the WR. Photograph B. Richardson, The Transport Treasury.

A Somerset and Dorset Class 5, 73050 at Bristol Temple Meads, 8 August 1954. This engine is now preserved as CITY OF PETERBOROUGH on the Nene Valley Railway. Photograph J. Robertson, The Transport Treasury.

73058 at Polmadie, 19 March 1955. In *The Stanier 4-6-0s of the LMS* (D&C, 1977) J.W.P. Rowledge and Brian Reed make the fascinating point that the designers' efforts to reduce preparation time was to some extent wasted, because under agreements of the period the time allowed a driver was based on the heating surface of the locomotive, with the dividing line set at 1,500sq. ft.. Under this arrangement the rather bonkers situation came about whereby less time was allowed for a Midland three cylinder Compound with three drive lines, six inside eccentrics and any number of inaccessible other parts than for a new BR Class 5 specially designed with economy of preparation time in mind. Photograph J. Robertson, The Transport Treasury.

73062 amid the usual mouth-watering offerings at Polmadie shed in the middle 1950s. 73056 and another Class 5 are beyond with, behind, a shimmeringly clean BR 2-6-4T and a Stanier Pacific. The BR Class 5s had Timken roller bearings (apart from 73090-73099 which had SKF Parallel roller type); 'Mac' in 'The Standard 5 is Good' approved: *'I have never before travelled on an engine fitted with roller bearings, at least to the extent which exists on the standard design, and I had ideas on the subject. Such an engine should run more smoothly, it should also maintain speed on the level when coasting. Engine 73009 proved both of these contentions right. I was writing notes legibly (for me) standing on the footplate at over 60mph. When the engine was coasting on a comparatively level stretch, I clocked each ¼mile post for almost three minutes until the brake was applied for a 'slow' and there was practically no diminution of speed until the brake was applied. That gives some rough and ready indication of the riding capabilities of the new 5'.* Photograph J. Robertson, The Transport Treasury.

73150 at Dundee on 27 April 1957. Had there been more of a future in steam, then Caprotti gear would certainly have become near-universal. The rotary drive came from worm gearing enclosed in an axle-mounted box between the frames, transmitted by bevel gearing to cam boxes on top of each cylinder – so obvious in any side view like this. Photograph J. Robertson, The Transport Treasury.

73059 leaving Princes Street station, Edinburgh on 21 April 1956. Much is made of the way the Standards were 'rejected' on the Western and 'embraced' on the Eastern. The Scots just took to them quietly it would seem, grateful for strong substitutes for older pre-Group designs. And (though he was writing for the 'house journal') try these additional comments from 'Mac': *'The line of visibility is exceptionally good from both sides of the cab, and everything to make for comfort is there, the only things missing in up-to-the-minute design being electric lighting and the automatic train control apparatus, which is due not to lack of thought on the designer's part but (as everyone knows) to lack of capital.'* Photograph J. Robertson, The Transport Treasury.

73000
To traffic 12/4/51
Tender: Type BR1 No.794

SHEDS
Derby (loan) 28/4/51
Derby (transfer) 26/5/51
On Loan ER (Stratford) 31/10/51
Derby (returned from loan) 15/3/52
Millhouses 10/1/53
Derby 28/2/53
Nottingham 19/9/53
To ER, Grimesthorpe 20/4/58
Canklow ER 1/1/61
Derby (LMR) 31/12/61
Woodford Halse 21/9/62
Oxley 1/65
Shrewsbury 'To NW lines' 30/4/65
Agecroft 30/4/66
Stored 2/5/66 to 13/5/67

REPAIRS
13/4/51-24/4/51, painting, Derby
26/6/51-2/7/51, drawgear, Derby
4/10/51-19/10/51, Piston &Valve liners, Derby
22/4/52-20/5/52, Cylinders, Derby
12/8/53-10/9/53**I** Derby
25/5/54-17/6/54**I** Derby
21/9/54-21/10/54**LC** Derby
17/1056-16/11/56**G** Derby
2/12/57-3/1/58**LC** Derby
9/12/58-22/1/59**HI** Doncaster Mileage 81,826
11/9/61-29/12/61**G** Doncaster
16/6/65-6/9/65**LI** Cowlairs
Condemned 3/68. Stored Patricroft shed; cut up at Cashmores, Great Bridge, 6/68

73082 CAMELOT
Named w/e 15/8/59 at Eastleigh Works
Tender: Type BR1D No.1208.
Steam operated cylinder cocks; piston head ring grooves deepened; modified blowdown valve gear to H.O.9216.

SHEDS
Stewarts Lane 6/55
Nine Elms 5/59
Guildford 5/65

REPAIRS
28/12/55-17/2/56**LC** Crewe
28/10/57-30/11/57**LI-HI** Eastleigh 95,815[1]
28/7/59-15/8/59**LI** Eastleigh 165,514[2]
4/3/60-19/3/60**LC** Eastleigh 184,858
5/12/60-24/12/60**LC** Eastleigh 212,988
1/8/61-2/9/61**G** Eastleigh 236,978[3]
15/11/63-21/12/63**LI** Eastleigh 88,519[4]

[1]T2263(O). Blowdown valvegear, safety links between engine and tender.
[2]Injector overflow pipes and brackets; isolating cock; nameplate fitted.
[3]Tender coalhole door plates.
[4]AWS gear made operative.

73153
To traffic 24 May 1957
Fitted with Caprotti valve gear
AWS
Tender: Type BR1B No.1441

SHEDS
St.Rollox 5/57
Stirling 11/66

REPAIRS
4/2/59-27/2/59**LI** Cowlairs
4/7/60-15/7/60**LC(EO)** Cowlairs
11/1/61-18/2/61**G** Cowlairs
27/11/61-20/12/61**LC(EO)** Cowlairs
8/11/62-1/12/62**LC(EO)** Cowlairs
4/6/63-15/6/63**LC(EO)** Cowlairs
25/3/64-1/5/64**LC(EO)** Cowlairs
13/5/64-20/5/64**NC(EO)** Cowlairs
25/6/64-15/7/64**LC(EO)** Cowlairs
14/12/64-26/12/64**LC(EO)** Cowlairs
11/1/65-16/2/65**NC(EO)** Cowlairs
3/2/66-5/3/66 **LC(EO)** Cowlairs
Condemned 9/12/66; stored Stirling shed 11/66-3/67
Scrapped Shipbreaking Industries, Faslane, 4/67

A '5' in the rain, 73096 blowing off and waiting for the signal at Shrewsbury in the 1950s. This is a good view, despite the conditions, of the big nine ton BR1C tender, which gave an altogether more hard-nosed air to the '5'. 73096 is now preserved on the Mid-Hants Railway and has also performed on the main line. Photograph The Transport Treasury.

Left. That distinctive 'BR' front end, unmistakable amongst British locomotive design. Many found it too utilitarian by far, yet the Standards carried on the 'clean lines' tradition of British practice and were sleek indeed compared to other country's designs. One is proud of British locomotive appearance, naturally, but it's hard not to hanker after at least one mad confection of domes, valves, pipes, pumps and rodding after the fashion, of say, the French. (Irwell Press tell me this is as far as I can go.) The date of this photograph is not known but it would be about 1962. At least we know the location; 75013 is, demonstrably, at Sandy and, carrying a Bletchley 1E shedplate (it was there from April 1962 to June 1965) must be on one of those wonderful, interminable workings on the old LNW route between (Oxford), Bletchley, Bedford and Cambridge. The passenger work had been in the hands of multiple units as early as 1960. Photograph The Transport Treasury.

Below. With the establishment of the BR Board at its Marylebone HQ ('the Kremlin') it became the custom to show locomotives at the station close by, so that the Board members had just a short stroll before a good lunch, or a trial trip to Princes Risborough, say, for an even nicer lunch. From *Railway Observer* notes, this occasion would be 23 May 1951, when the 'Fell' diesel (behind 75000, with its access doors open) was towed to Marylebone by 75000. That's 73001 (73000 had been on display here earlier in the year, on 26 April) in front of 75000; 70009 ALFRED THE GREAT was also in the line-up and there were coaches and wagons on view as well.

The 'New Manors'

75050 on 21 August 1957, leaving Earlestown for Manchester. The 4MT 4-6-0, as Cox relates in *British Railways Standard Steam Locomotives*, came about as a more far-ranging (through increased coal and water capacity) version of the 2-6-4T for more remote areas which precluded a Class 5 on the grounds of weight. It was the sort of niche occupied on the WR by the little Manor 4-6-0s, which could not roam further afield because of the width over cylinders. The range of twelve standard classes have often been spoken of in terms of 'over-egging the pudding' but the more you look at them in detail (remember, it was generally considered that steam still had a good thirty years to go) the more admirable this comprehensive interlocking fleet of engines – a modern type for every job in every situation – becomes. Photograph Les Elsey.

75003, one of the Western Region Class 4 4-6-0s, at Eastleigh on 16 August 1960, a few weeks after its transfer to Tyseley from Worcester. Conversions to double chimney had begun with 75029 in 1957 and though it was the intention that all the class should be so treated the work was only carried out on the SR ones and a few WR examples. The 75000 4-6-0s were subject to one of the oddest teething troubles ever known – 'groaning brake blocks'. These affected the Accrington allocation (75040-75049) so much that residents complained to *the police* about one early morning turn, such that a Crab had to be borrowed from Rose Grove. If or how this was ever resolved is not recorded. Photograph W. Hermiston, The Transport Treasury.

Table 1. Summary of British Railways Standard Steam Locomotive Boilers built 1950-1962

Prog.	BR	Nos.	Builder	Building dates 0 = uncertain	Class	For Loco Nos. (Builder)
Pre-1951	*10*	*1 - 757*	*NBL, VF*	*1942 - 1945*	*WD 2-8-0*	*90000-90732 + 24 spares*
	10	*758 - 775**	*Crewe*	*12.51 - 4.52*	*WD 2-8-0*	*For spare*
	11	*776 - 800*	*NBL*	*1943 - 1945*	*WD 2-10-0*	*90750-90774*
1951	1	801 - 825	Crewe	11.50 - 6.51	7 4-6-2	70000-70024(C)
	2	826 - 835	Crewe	10.51 - 6.51	6 4-6-2	72000-72009(C)
	3	836 - 865	Crewe	12.50 - 12.51	5 4-6-0	73000-73029(C)
	4	866 - 885	Swindon	4.51 - 8.51	4 4-6-0	75000-75019 (SW)
	5	886 - 895	Crewe	2.52 – 6.52	4 2-6-4T	80000-80009 (DY)
	5	896 - 929 evens odds	Eastleigh Brighton	5.51 – 10.52 6.51 – 5.52	Ditto	80010-80043 (B)
	5	930 - 939	Brighton	5.51 – 10.52	Ditto	80044-80053(B)
	6	940 - 959	Swindon	12.51 – 7.52	3 2-6-2T	82000-82019 (SW)
Spares	*11*	*960**	*Crewe*	*3.52*	*WD 2-10-0*	*To Scottish Region*
	1	961 - 963*	Crewe	5.53 – 3.54	7 4-6-2	(Crewe)
	2	964*	Crewe	9.55	6 4-6-2	(Crewe)
	3	965 - 966*	Crewe	1.54 – 2.54	5 4-6-0	To Derby
	5	967*	Crewe	1.56	4 2-6-4T	To Derby
1952	1	973 - 992	Crewe	6.52 – 10.52	7 4-6-2	70025-70044(C)
	3	993 - 1012	Crewe	4.53 – 10.53	5 4-6-0	73030-73049(DY)
	4	1013 - 1042	Swindon	3.53 – 3.54	4 4-6-0	75020 – 75049(SW)
	7	1043 - 1052	Darlington	5.52 – 11.52	4 2-6-0	76000-76009(H)
	7	1053 - 1062	Doncaster	0.52 – 0.52	Ditto	76010-76019(H)
	7	1063 - 1067	Doncaster	0.52 – 11.52	Ditto	76020-76024(DON)
	8	1068 - 1077	Darlington	12.52 – 4.53	2 2-6-0	78000-78009(DAR)
	5	1078 - 1082	Crewe	11.54	4 2-6-4T	80054-80058(DY)
	5	1083-1092	Brighton	0.53 – 8.53	Ditto	80059-80068(B)
	6	1093 - 1107	Swindon	5.54 – 9.54	3 2-6-2T	82020-82034(SW)
	8	1108 - 1127	Crewe	3.53 – 9.53	2 2-6-2T	84000-84019(C)
1953	9	1128 - 1147	Crewe	10.53 – 8.54	9F 2-10-0	92000-92019(C)
	12	1148 - 1157	Crewe	2.55 – 5.55	Ditto (Crosti)	92020-92029(C)
	1	1158 - 1167	Crewe	4.54 – 11.54	7 4-6-2	70045-70054(C)
	3	1168 - 1192	Crewe	1.54 – 11.54	5 4-6-0	73050-73074(DY)
	4	1193 - 1207	Swindon	4.56 – 4.57	4 4-6-0	75050-75064(SW)
	4	1208 - 1222	Swindon	5.55 – 12.55	Ditto	75065-75079(SW)
	7	1223 - 1242	Doncaster	8.53 – 0.54	4 2-6-0	76025-76044(DON)
	6	1243 - 1262	Swindon	11.53 – 4.54	3 2-6-0	77000-77019(SW)
	8	1263 - 1297	Darlington	12.53 – 12.54	2 2-6-0	78010-78044(DAR)
	5	1298 – 1334	Brighton	0.53 – 0.55	4 2-6-4T	80069-80105(B)
	5	1335 - 1344	Doncaster	10.54 – 0.55	Ditto	80106-80115(DON)
	6	1345 - 1354	Swindon	1.55 – 3.55	3 2-6-2T	82035-82044(SW)
	8	1355 - 1364	Darlington	3.57 – 6.57	2 2-6-2T	84020-84029(DAR)
Spares	1	1365 – 1366*	Crewe	1.55 – 2.55	7 4-6-2	(Crewe)
	3	1367*	Crewe	2.54	5 4-6-0	To Derby
	5	1368*	Crewe	5.57	4 2-6-4T	To Derby
	8	1369*	Crewe	9.56	2 2-6-2T	(Crewe)
	4	1370 – 1374*	Swindon	9.55 – 10.55	4 4-6-0	(Swindon)
	6	1375 – 1379*	Swindon	10.55 – 1.56	Class 3	(Swindon 3) to Darlington (1) and Eastleigh (1)
	10	*1380 - 1409**	*Crewe*	*9.53 – 7.54*	*WD 2-8-0*	
1954	9	1410 - 1466	Crewe	9.54 – 6.56	9F 2-10-0	92030-92086(C)
	9	1467 - 1476	Swindon	5.56 – 2.57	Ditto	92087-92096(SW)
	(2)	(1477 – 1491)	(Crewe)	Cancelled 4.55	(6 4-6-2)	(72010-72024)
	3	1492 - 1506	Crewe	3.55 – 8.55	5 4-6-0	73075-73089(DY)
	(4)	(1507 – 1516)	(Swindon)	Cancelled 9.56	(4 4-6-0)	(75080-75089)
	7	1517 - 1546	Doncaster	3.55 – 6.57	4 2-6-0	76045-76074(DON)
	(6)	(1547 – 1551)	(Swindon)	Cancelled 9.56	(3 2-6-0)	(77020-77024)
	8	1552 - 1561	Darlington	10.55 – 12.55	2 2-6-0	78045-78054(DAR)
	5	1562 - 1576	Brighton	0.55	4 2-6-4T	80116-80130(B)
	(6)	(1577 – 1594)	Swindon	Cancelled 9.56	(3 2-6-2T)	(82045-82062)
Spares	4	1595 – 1597*	Swindon	5.56	4 4-6-0	To Derby
	5	1598*	Crewe	5.59	4 2-6-4T	Ditto
	5	1599*	Brighton	11.55	Ditto	(Brighton)
	7	1600*	Doncaster	12.54	4 2-6-0	To Eastleigh
	8	1601 – 1602*	Crewe	1.58 – 9.58	2 2-6-2T	(Crewe)
	13	1603	Crewe	2.54	8 4-6-2	71000(C) (special order)
	7	1604 – 1605*	Doncaster	3.56	4 2-6-0	To Eastleigh
	3	1606*	Crewe	3.55	5 4-6-0	To Derby
	5	1607 – 1608*	Crewe	5.56 – 6.56	4 2-6-4T	To St Rollox
1955	3	1609 - 1618	Crewe	9.55 – 11.55	5 4-6-0	73090–73099(DY)
	3	1619 - 1628	Darlington	6.55 – 11.55	Ditto	73100– 3109(DON)
	3	1629 - 1638	Doncaster	10.55 – 0.56	Ditto	73110–73119(DON)
	3	1639 - 1643	Darlington	4.55 – 6.55	Ditto	73120–73124(DON)
1956	9	1644 - 1724	Crewe	5.56 – 1.58	9F 2-10-0	92097-92177(C)
	9	1725 - 1749	Swindon	6.57 – 10.58	Ditto	92178-92202(SW)
	3	1750 - 1779	Crewe	12.55 – 11.56	5 4-6-0	73125-73154(DY)
	3	1780 - 1796	Darlington	10.56 – 4.57	Ditto	73155-73171(DON)
	7	1797 - 1821	Swindon	8.56 – 9.57	4 2-6-0	76075-76099(H)
	7	1822 - 1831	Darlington	8.56 – 10.56	Ditto	76100-76109(DON)
	7	1832 - 1836	Doncaster	8.57 – 11.57	Ditto	76110-76114(DON)
	8	1837 - 1846	Darlington	8.56 – 11.56	2 2-6-0	78055-78064(DAR)
	5	1847 - 1870	Brighton	0.56 – 2.57	4 2-6-4T	80131-80154(B)
Spares	3	1871*	Crewe	3.57	5 4-6-0	To Eastleigh
	5	1872*	Brighton	4.57	4 2-6-4T	To Darlington
	6	1873*	Swindon	1.60	3 2-6-0	To Wolverhampton
	7	1874*	Doncaster	4.57	4 2-6-0	To Eastleigh
	8	1875*	Darlington	10.56	2 2-6-0	(Darlington)
	9	1876 –1877*	Crewe	5.57 – 9.57	9F 2-10-0	To Darlington, (Swindon)
	11	*1878**	*NBL*	*1945 (2nd hand)*	*WD 2-10-0*	
1957	9	1879 - 1896	Swindon	12.58 – 11.59	9F 2-10-0	92203-92220(SW)
Spares	3	1897-1898*	Crewe	3.59	5 4-6-0	To Cowlairs
	7	1899 – 1900*	Crewe	10.59 – 1.60	4 2-6-0	To Cowlairs
	9	1901 – 1902*	Crewe	2.59	9F 2-10-0	(Crewe)
	12	1903*	Crewe	10.61	Ditto	(Crewe)
	1	1904*	Crewe	5.59	7 4-6-2	To Swindon
	3	1905 – 1906*	Darlington	12.58	5 4-6-0	To Doncaster, Eastleigh
	9	1907*	Crewe	5.59	9F 2-10-0	(Crewe)
	9	1908*	Swindon	5.60	Ditto	(Swindon)
	3	1909 – 1911*	Crewe	10.59 –1.60	5 4-6-0	To Swindon (2), Derby (1)
1958	9	1912 - 1941	Crewe	1.58 – 11.58	9F 2-10-0	92221-92250(C)
1959	5	1942*	Eastleigh	11.61	4 2-6-4T	(Eastleigh)
Spares	7	1943*	Doncaster	9.59	4 2-6-0	To Eastleigh
	9	1944 – 1945*	Crewe	6.61 – 7.61	9F 2-10-0	(Crewe)
	9	1946 – 1947*	Swindon	3.60 – 4.60	Ditto	(Swindon)
1960	6	1948*	Swindon	3.61	3 2-6-0	To Cowlairs
Spares	8	1949*	Crewe	12.60	2 2-6-0	To Cowlairs
	9	1950 – 1951*	Crewe	3.62 – 5.62	9F 2-10-0	(Crewe)

* Denotes boilers built under spares programmes

B = Brighton, C = Crewe, DAR = Darlington, DON = Doncaster, DY = Derby, E = Eastleigh, H = Horwich, SW = Swindon, NBL = North British Locomotive Company, Glasgow, VF = Vulcan Foundry, Newton-le-Willows, Lancs.

For consistency building date is *effective* completion date, which includes mounting, which is only given in Swindon records, whereas Crewe records quote building and mounting dates. Brighton, Darlington and Doncaster records give only a nominal date. Normally mounting closely followed building, but a notable exception was BR3/1911 which was built at Crewe in 1959, but not sent to Derby until three years later, where it was mounted and put onto 73011 in December 1962, making it the last BR Standard boiler to enter service. BR12/1903 was built without the pre-heater because by this time the Crostis had nearly all been converted to conventional operation. Note it would originally have been authorised about *six* years earlier!

A NOTE ON BRITISH RAILWAYS STANDARD STEAM LOCOMOTIVE BOILERS

By Philip Atkins

For the 999 Standards a total of 1,066 boilers (999+67 spares) was built, the last at Crewe, two years after the emergence of No.92220 from Swindon, and therefore only shortly before withdrawal of the Standards commenced later in 1962. Of the seven BR Works which erected the Standards, only five built boilers for them. The exceptions were Derby and Horwich but Eastleigh, which built no Standards, made a few boilers for Brighton. The boilers themselves were built in batches which (in theory) corresponded with the batches of Standards built under annual locomotive building programmes. These were supplemented by spares, built to provide a float in order to facilitate repairs, which were built under separate annual spare locomotive boiler programmes. Like the building programmes the spare boiler programmes quickly slipped and the time of a boiler's construction often differed completely from the intended year.

Although often boilers were sequentially attached as planned, this did not always happen. Boilers for 'new build' were sometimes put on out of sequence, or might be put on to an older engine back in works for heavy repair. Conversely a 'spare' boiler might be put onto a new engine. In the case of the boiler originally scheduled for No.92220 this was actually shipped from Swindon to Darlington where it was put onto two year old No.92180.

The BR Standard boiler numbering system also embraced the ex-War Department 'Austerity' 2-8-0s and 2-10-0s, for which there happened to be a combined total of boilers, including spares, of precisely 800 in 1950. The Standards 'proper' therefore commenced at 801 and eventually concluded at 1,951. This number range included 48 allotted to the engines on the 1954 Programme which were subsequently cancelled and a number of spare boilers for the WD 2-8-0s and 2-10-0s which were built at Crewe during 1951-54.

The boiler types were coded BR1 to BR13. BR1, 2, 9, 12 and 13, all with wide fireboxes, were all entirely new designs, although somewhat inter-related. BR3, 5, 7 and 8 were almost direct copies of former LMS antecedents. BR4 was a development of BR5, while BR6 was based on the former GWR Standard No.2 boiler. BR6 and 8 were each employed on both 2-6-0 tender and their 2-6-2 tank engine equivalents, occasionally passing from a tender to a tank engine and vice versa. BR10 and 11 were the parallel round-topped boilers fitted to the WD 2-8-0s and 2-10-0s. The unique boiler number, in the form 'BRx/1234', was inscribed on a small brass tablet mounted on the centre of the firebox backplate. As with the BR Standard locomotives themselves (pre-preservation) boiler life varied from 17 years down to only five years, or possibly even less. Records are not complete, especially after about 1960 and particularly with respect to the Scottish Region, although boiler changes occurred with ever-decreasing frequency until late 1966. No.70000 and several of the first fifteen Class 7 4-6-2s certainly carried five (and some of them possibly even six) different boilers, but at the other extreme some of the later Standards, including No.92220, never underwent a boiler change at all.

Table 2. British Railways Standard Spare Steam Locomotive Boilers and Their Disposition.

Boiler No.	Builder	Date	Sent to	Fitted to	Date
1/961	Crewe	5.53	(Crewe)	70021	6.53
1/962	Ditto	6.53	Ditto	70047 (new engine)	(6.54)
1/963	Ditto	3.54	Ditto	70045 (new engine)	(7.54)
2/964	Ditto	9.55	Ditto	72007	10.55
3/965	Ditto	1.54	Derby 2.54	73052 (new engine)	(6.54)
3/966	Ditto	2.54	Ditto 2.54	Not recorded	-
5/967	Ditto	1.56	Ditto 1.56	80085	1.57
1/1365	Ditto	1.55	(Crewe)	70001	2.55
1/1366	Ditto	2.55	Ditto	70007	5.55
3/1367	Ditto	2.54	Derby 2.54	Not recorded	-
5/1368	Ditto	5.57	Ditto 5.57	80045	8.57
8/1369	Ditto	9.56	(Crewe)	84001	12.57
4/1370	Swindon	9.55	(Swindon)	75075 (new engine)	(11.55)
4/1371	Ditto	10.55	Ditto	75076 (new engine)	(12.55)
4/1372	Ditto	10.55	Ditto	75000	12.55
4/1373	Ditto	10.55	Ditto	75008	12.56
4/1374	Ditto	10.55	Ditto	75006	9.56
6/1375	Ditto	10.55	Ditto	82000	10.56
6/1376	Ditto	11.55	Darlington 10.56	77001	3.57
6/1377	Ditto	11.55	(Swindon)	82007	12.56
6/1378	Ditto	12.55	Ditto	82004	2.57
6/1379	Ditto	1.56	Eastleigh 11.56	82019	3.57
4/1595	Ditto	5.56	Derby	75014	10.56
4/1596	Ditto	5.56	Ditto	75015	11.56
4/1597	Ditto	5.56	Ditto	75010	11.56
5/1598	Crewe	5.59	Ditto 5.59	80093	11.59
5/1599	Brighton	11.55	Brighton	80019	8.56
7/1600	Doncaster	12.54	Eastleigh	76009	5.57
8/1601	Crewe	9.58	(Crewe)	84007	9.58
8/1602	Ditto	1.58	Ditto	84006	4.58
7/1604	Doncaster	3.56	Uncertain	76068	3.56
7/1605	Ditto	3.56	Eastleigh	76050	?
3/1606	Crewe	3.55	Derby 5.55	73083 (new engine)	(7.55)
5/1607	Ditto	5.56	St Rollox 5.56	80021	9.56
5/1608	Ditto	6.56	Ditto 6.56	80023	4.57
3/1871	Crewe	3.57	Eastleigh 3.57	73041	11.58
5/1872	Brighton	4.57	Darlington 11.57	80099	3.58
6/1873	Swindon	1.60	Wolverhampton	82005	6.60
7/1874	Doncaster	4.57	Eastleigh	76005	6.57
8/1875	Darlington	0.56	(Darlington)	78016	10.56
9/1876	Crewe	5.57	Ditto 5.57	92012	8.57
9/1877	Ditto	9.57	Swindon 9.57	92198 (new engine)	(9.58)
3/1897	Ditto	3.59	Cowlairs 3.59	Not recorded	-
3/1898	Ditto	3.59	Ditto 3.59	Ditto	-
7/1899	Ditto	10.59	Ditto 10.59	Ditto	-
7/1900	Ditto	1.60	Ditto 1.60	Ditto	-
9/1901	Ditto	2.59	(Crewe)	92009	4.59
9/1902	Ditto	2.59	Ditto	92136	1.60
12/1903	Ditto	10.61	Ditto	92024	11.61
1/1904	Ditto	5.59	Swindon 8.59	70028	10.60
3/1905	Darlington	0.58	Doncaster 12.58	73016	2.59
3/1906	Ditto	0.58	Eastleigh 12.58	73051	5.59
9/1907	Crewe	5.59	(Crewe)	92015	12.59
9/1908	Swindon	5.60	(Swindon)	92008	6.60
3/1909	Crewe	10.59	Ditto 11.59	73026	3.60
3/1910	Ditto	1.60	Ditto 1.60	73031	6.60
3/1911	Ditto	(7.59)	Derby 6.62	73011	12.62
5/1942	Eastleigh	11.61	(Eastleigh)	80149	1.62
7/1943	Doncaster	9.59	Ditto 9.59	76062	9.59
9/1944	Crewe	6.61	(Crewe)	92051	6.61
9/1945	Ditto	7.61	Ditto	92072	8.61
9/1946	Swindon	3.60	(Swindon)	92003	12.60
9/1947	Ditto	4.60	Ditto	92002	11.60
6/1948	Ditto	3.61	Cowlairs 4.61	Not recorded (2-6-0)	-
8/1949	Crewe	12.60	Ditto 12.60	Ditto (2-6-0)	-
9/1950	Ditto	5.62	(Crewe)	92093	5.62
9/1951	Ditto	3.62	Ditto	92045	4.62

The Airfix Moguls

76000 on the turntable at Polmadie, 20 March 1954. The burly Class 4 2-6-0s were built at Horwich and Doncaster and Airfix put a stirring painting of one on the box of its reissued Kitmaster kit in 1967. This, by the renowned Roy Cross showed the last one, 76114, on a turntable, much as we see it here. Take a look at the box again if you have one. As Stephen Knight points out in *Let's Stick Together* (Irwell Press, 1999) the normally assiduous artist overlooked the front coupling rod, depicting what was in fact a 2-2-4-0... 76000 had arrived in Scotland on 4 December 1952, on an afternoon freight from Kingmoor. On reaching Auchinleck it was promptly involved in a collision and ended up 'quite knocked about a bit'. This situation, of a new locomotive getting into such trouble on its first job, is probably unique. It went back to Horwich for treatment to the bent front end and was back in Scotland at the end of the year. In January 1953 another one was in trouble, 76002 being observed dead at York on its way back to Doncaster, with its motion piled up on the tender. Photograph J. Robertson, The Transport Treasury.

76001 at Motherwell in September 1955. It got as far as Kingmoor and then into Scotland in the time that its predecessor, 76000, was back at Horwich getting over its embarrassment. The first five, 76000-76004, all went to Motherwell. Photograph W. Hermiston, The Transport Treasury.

76011 brand new outside Horwich Works, 17 March 1953. The rest of Horwich's first batch of twenty were destined for the Southern Region and the next engines, 76005-76019, all went to Eastleigh. Photograph M.N. Bland, The Transport Treasury.

A pristine 76025 at Eastleigh shed on 12 August 1955. The first of the engines to come out of Doncaster, this had been one of five, 76025-76029, sent to Eastleigh in October 1953.

76030 (shown here at the approaches to Liverpool Street) was the first of the 'Airfix Moguls' on the Eastern Region, five (76030-76034) going new from Doncaster at the end of 1953. The Eastern Region got fifteen in all – most of the deliveries, from both Horwich and Doncaster seem to have been in fives or multiples thereof. 76030-76034 were at Stratford where they were more or less lost amid the sea of other types at the huge depot ('always in trouble' with staff shortages and so on). The other ten, 76035-76044 with rather more sense, were concentrated at Neasden. When that shed passed to the LM Stratford's five were the only ones on the Eastern Region; 76035-76044 had gone by default and Stratford's five were duly 'sent to the country' in 1960 in the maelstrom of Stratford's conversion to diesels. Like the Britannias and other engines marked for future use they were concentrated at March, transferring to the Southern Region en bloc in November 1962. Photograph Ted's Dad.

One of the Southern examples, 76061 at Brighton on 31 July 1955. Only 76053-76069 had the high sided (Type 1B) tenders and a huge difference it made to the looks of the engines. Photograph The Transport Treasury.

76114, the last of the class, the 2,228th and last steam engine built at Doncaster and star of the Airfix box, new on 17 October 1957. Doncaster carried on repairing steam locomotives, building new Pacific boilers until 1961 and not finally ending steam repairs until 1963. The last Horwich steam locomotive was also one of the Class 4 2-6-0s, 76099 a few weeks later on 29 November. Thus completed in 1957, the 76000s only had seven years as a complete class, the first one going in May 1964.

76063 with high 1B tender, at Eastleigh shed on 16 August 1960. The Class 4 2-6-0s were one of the Standards that were simply LMS types amended to take standard fittings. The BR Class 4 was in all vital respects the Ivatt Class 4, to the extent that the stationary tests for the class were done using 43094. Photograph W. Hermiston, The Transport Treasury.

The Mighty Midgets

The little 77000 Moguls were to many the ugliest and gawkiest of the Standards but to others they were elegant and fascinating. Perhaps it was a question of being trapped in the south, with these engines seldom coming within 200-odd miles of one's pencil and notebook. They never seem to have made much of a mark (certainly nothing to compare with 77014's much later impact on the Southern in 1966-67) which is hardly surprising. They were, after all, plonked down in very small quantities amid any number of existing Class 3 and 4 locomotives. Inevitably they found themselves on Class 4 duties in which enginemen, equally inevitably, found them underpowered. With that they would be damned without hope of redemption. 77000 and the next four (batches of five again, be it noted) went new to Darlington and thereafter all moved extensively around North Eastern Region sheds. 77000 in this picture is at Darlington shed, having moved back there after its travels for the second time in January 1963. It went to its final shed, Stourton, in 1964 and was withdrawn at the end of 1966. Photograph The Transport Treasury.

A pretty picture capturing the elegance of these little locos, at Farnley Junction on 1 May 1964. 77001 had moved here at the end of the previous year. It is actually on the coaling road; that's the ash plant beyond, on the other side of the triangle around the shed, the offices and roofs of which are visible beyond the coal wagons. Photograph The Transport Treasury.

77005 the first of three, 77005, 77006 and 77007, to go new to Hamilton. The date is given as July 1954 but there is no location. Would it be Glasgow Central? The 77000s had the revised cab arrangement from the first, together with other later features such as plain section coupling rods and speedo. Photograph C.L. Kerr, The Transport Treasury.

77009 more or less new at Swindon Works on 25 April 1954. It was new to traffic in June. Swindon of course, if you lived in the south east, was the nearest place to see the 77000s, though no photographs seem to exist of them on trials down to Exeter or on their journeys north to their homes. At this time, when 77009 was being finished at Swindon in April 1954, 77007 and 77008 were noted on up goods trains through Gloucester on 21 and 28 April respectively and 77007 on a Swindon to Bristol train on 10 May. 77006 had been to Plymouth twice on fish trains (a favourite – see the first *Book of the BR Standards*) while on 8 May 77008 passed through Banbury on its way to Scotland. Someone must have photographed one of them! Photograph M.N. Bland, The Transport Treasury.

77009 was presumably the first and only – until 1966 – Class 3 to visit London, being sent up in suitable sparkling condition for the International Railway Congress Exhibition at Willesden shed in 1954. On going north to Perth in June it was put out at Blair Atholl to work as a banker. It was decidedly *not* the sort of work envisaged by the design team and it was the low mileages resulting from this sort of thing (using Class 2 Moguls on Officer's Specials, station pilots and suchlike) that alerted 'high up'. The problem was that, in a situation that did not require excessive work at least, the new engines were just too comfy... Photograph J. Robertson, The Transport Treasury.

77010 at Scarborough on 10 July 1954. As is well recorded, the boiler, like that for the Class 3 2-6-2T, was the GW design used on the 5101 2-6-2Ts, among others. Photograph The Transport Treasury.

77011 at Blaydon shed, 26 May 1956. The Mighty Midgets as a species were up a'gin it. There were plenty of Class 2, 3 and 4 0-6-0s to do the jobs, there were rarely more than two or three at any given shed and the sort of branch/colliery trip work for which they were so suited was disappearing – as were the lightly laid branches which could not bear anything greater than the 16 ton 77000 axleload. Photograph A.G. Ellis, The Transport Treasury.

77013, in typical 'high stepping' pose, at Darlington on 31 July 1955. When 77014 came at the last down to the Southern she soon looked at home amid the other Standards. The SR certainly found plenty of work for it and it was on a parcels on the very last weekend of Southern steam in July 1967 – a thousand pities that it didn't end up at Barry for eventual rescue. It was certainly a telling sign of the times; 77014 went down for a special and just 'stayed'. Northwich, it seemed, could hardly be bothered to ask for it back! Photograph A.G. Ellis, The Transport Treasury.

Moguls, Old Style

The little Class 2 2-6-0s were the same engines built by the LMS and BR in the 6400/46400 series but with external detail differences. This mainly concerned the cab which now lent inwards a little to give them a rather better range. 78011 and 78014 are at Northallerton shed on 1 August 1955, two of the five (78010-78014) transferred from West Auckland at the behest of Mr G.C. Bird, formerly Shedmaster at Kirkby Stephen (see *Book of the BR Standards*). Photograph A.G. Ellis, The Transport Treasury.

It was natural that the Class 2 Moguls should find themselves in districts like rural Wales where good steaming and reliability, light axleload, comfortable cabs and good water and coal capacity were so useful – though Class 3 2-6-0s might have been a better bet. Several were at Machynlleth, including 78002 which, on 10 July 1954 was on a train at Afon Wen, together with 2-6-2T 4560. Afon Wen was a curious place, remote by the sea shore with only an unmade road to the outside world and with seals as often as not lazing on rocks just offshore. On summer Saturdays in particular it came alive with complex and often heavy holiday traffic, especially when the LM line in from Caernarvon was still working. The Butlin's Penychain camp opened in 1947 and was a major stimulus to all this throughout the 1950s. So far as I can work out the two locos are on a train to the camp; this view is looking east, back to Dovey Junction and the happy campers have only minutes to go. Well, that's my guess; the lack of grinning faces from the carriages might indicate something else. Empty stock? Photograph A.G. Ellis, The Transport Treasury.

A Class 2 in Scotland. 78050 at Motherwell on 2 June 1957. Typically a batch of five (78050-78054) had come here, at the very end of 1955. Curiously, no less than three of them, 78050, 78051 and 78052, despite moving in the meantime as far afield as Dumfries and even Aviemore, 'came home' to be scrapped, a short way off at the Motherwell Machinery Co, in 1966. Photograph W. Hermiston, The Transport Treasury.

It was a surprise to see a swathe of 78000s coming south near the end, for empty stock work out of Euston. Fifteen or so were eventually available and they became a familiar sight in the last year or two – three are outside Willesden shed in this view of about 1965, all now equipped with AWS (note the running plate battery boxes and air reservoirs). At the end, in September 1965, those with some life still left in them were sent away in pairs to Nuneaton leaving four dead amongst the debris, doomed to sit there with a handful of Stanier engines on into the winter. One was 78043, the middle engine in this picture. As mentioned in *The Book of the BR Standards* it was found that the 2MTs, especially, were being put on station pilot duties, in the main for the comfort of crews in winter and this began to throw up some puzzlingly low mileages. Orders went out to stop the practice but it's hard to see how it could have been enforced. The 'comfy cab' of the 78000s was doubtless a factor in choosing them for the Euston ECS jobs, which notoriously involved a lot of 'waiting about'. Photograph Dr Ian C. Allen, The Transport Treasury.

The front end of 70014 gives a splendid impression of power as he waits to cross over to take coal – something which would not have pleased me after the engine had been properly cleaned. Stewarts Lane Junction box is visible under the bridge which carries the old SECR main line by means of any number of permutations from Victoria down to Dover. The old SER and LCDR combined to ensure that Kent still has the most complex railway network in the country, maybe in the world. Photograph R.C. Riley, The Transport Treasury.

SPECIALISED WORK

The 'Shakespeare' and the 'Iron Duke'
By Richard Hardy

During my time as Shedmaster at Stewarts Lane from August 1952-January 1955, we had two Britannias, the 'Shakespeare' and the 'Iron Duke', 70004 and 70014, both very good engines well liked by all concerned especially by the maintenance staff and the stores people. The enginemen were very loyal to most of their original Bulleids which on their day had the same touch of genius as the man who had conceived them. 70004 was our regular engine for the 'Golden Arrow' (duty 4) which left the shed at 10.10 (summer time) in charge of Dover men off the 'Blue'. (The 'Blue' was the universal name at Stewarts Lane for the 'Night Ferry'; we even had a passenger train, '7pm, cuvver the Blue'.) 70004 was wiped over each day and it looked a mess yet this was the engine that worked the most glamorous train on BR. 70014 looked even worse, a disgrace to the shed. But in September 1952, the Arrow was retimed to leave Victoria at 14.00 (summer time) for Folkestone Junction and Harbour. Having turned at the Junction and after the fireman had built a good back end with the excellent briquettes off the coal stage, (the normal diet of the R1 tanks that worked the Harbour Branch) 70004 took the empties to Dover for the up 'Arrow' which left at 17.58 and was allowed ninety-two minutes to reach Victoria. If the boat was late or there was an exceptional number of passengers through the customs, the train would have to wait for one of the booked alternative paths. These were mostly up the main via Tonbridge but the third alternative was, I think, up the 'Chatham'. On Sunday there was a path up the 'Maidstone East' which was most unpopular with crew and passengers alike although, scenically, it was a lovely road.

However, 70004 now worked the train both ways in charge of men in No.1, the Boat train link which was as it should be. They came on duty at 12.35, prepared the engine and left at 13.35 for 14.00 from Victoria. The up train was due in at 19.30 and provided that there was no 'weaseling', it would soon be on its way to Stewarts Lane, banked by 70004. On arrival the engine went straight to the shed to be left for disposal on the coal road. The crew would therefore finish within eight hours and be paid mileage for the 158 miles. What did not go down at all well was when the train was held at Victoria while those who should have been clearing it were 'weaseling' (carrying baggage for passengers) while the enginemen were 'Working for the Queen'. Once the day was calculated on the mileage basis, no overtime was paid so the crew would get the same whether they worked eight hours or their day was frittered away over at Victoria.

The best five cleaners available saw to 70004 with time to clean, scour and polish the engine daily to bring it to the state of perfection required to exceed the splendour of the Pullman train. 70014 worked the second 'Arrow' (duty 5) to Dover half an hour later and acted as standby in case of last minute failure which was a rarity. If 70004 was laid off or 'shed', a 'nobbed-up' MN or BoB with a large tender, such as 35028 or 34071, would be booked and kept

The down Golden Arrow near Shorncliffe coasting down to Folkestone Junction and the dead end near Martello tunnel, on 7 August 1956. The R1 0-6-0Ts will couple up and take the train down the 1 in 30 to the Harbour while 'The Shakespeare', 70004, crosses over to the coal stage in the Junction 'Loco'. The crew will fill the back end of the big firebox with those excellent Welsh briquettes which will cook and make a good body of fire against the long drag up to Sandling on the return Arrow from Dover. Two summers have all but passed since I left the Lane. The train is lighter by at least one Pullman, the brightwork is no longer polished on 70004, for there are few cleaners available but she is passably clean. The fireman is relaxing but he has a shade too much fire, the blower is eased back and the safety valves may well lift before long. It was impossible to keep the smokebox top clean as the exhaust when running easily was sucked ahead of the chimney. Photograph R.C. Riley, The Transport Treasury.

Driver Bill Johnson in No.4, the spare link, is on the job on 27 February 1957. His fireman has put the tail lamp in place with the disc board ready for when they reach Victoria. Bill is waiting to cross over to the coal road. In the background are two Battersea engines. On the left is N class 31412 carrying the headcode for Battersea Yard to Portsmouth via Redhill and Horsham. It was one of the last Ns to be built, with left-hand drive. The regulator linkage was never altered from that required for right-hand drive, so that the handle had to moved downwards to open and lifted to close. Charlie Sinden wrote to me: 'Before your time when I was firing to young Fred Smith, we were the Eardley shunting engine with 1414 in 14 road so I told Fred who said "I'll be round in a minute". So I goes round and takes the hand brake off and puts her in back gear and – wallop – I started to move and hit another engine and when Fred came the regulator was wide open, the cylinder cocks closed and the front end knocked out. Fred got some story going and we all took some of the blame, the fitter, boilerwasher and firelighter.' On the right is 'Converted Coppertop' class E1 31067, a 52 ton world beater. Photograph R.C. Riley, The Transport Treasury.

Bill Johnson has his coal and all is ready for him to move, by easy stages, into 'Stew Lane' yard where he will be attached to the rear of the Pullman empties and so to Victoria. The engine looks quite smart but look at the left-hand cylinder cover. Photograph R.C. Riley, The Transport Treasury.

Dover Marine with what had been the Lord Warden Hotel in the background. On the right can be seen the crossing gates to the Marine; Hawksbury Street signalbox is on the far side of the old LCDR line to Victoria via Faversham and Chatham. In the autumn of 1956, three months before 70004 went to Crewe for a General Repair, Driver Bill Murray has worked the Arrow empties from Folkestone Junction tender first, run round the train and is now going into Dover shed until about twenty minutes before train time at 17.58. The flags are brand new and put on a brave show. The Lord Warden was opened in 1851 on land which the SER was obliged to buy. It was not put to use until the Harbour Commissioners insisted that the SER built its hotel on the foreshore, which was far from its original intention. But the Lord Warden became a legendary rendezvous for travellers from all over the world until the Second World War. Photograph R.C. Riley, The Transport Treasury.

there until 70004 returned to the charge. Only in the summer could we get two rounds to the coast and back on boat train duty so the mileage of our two 7MTs stood no comparison with those on other Regions. But the work they were required to do was consistently hard, nothing less than 420-480 tons boat trains over the most complex, heavily graded and difficult road out of any London terminus on any Region. It was all over pretty quickly but it was hard going for the stoker.

Given 230-250psi in the boiler, our two engines had all the guts in the world. To hear the old 'Shakespeare' roar up into the 80s with every exhaust sharp and distinct was a joy and they could be heard a long way away but hard work never disturbed the firebed

27 July 1957, and there have been some changes. The Golden Arrow train runs to seven Pullman; three corridor coaches, the customary luggage van and the 'fourgons' in the rear for registered luggage to be transferred direct to the ship. There are changes on 70004 since she went through Crewe Works. They have nicked the long lamp irons, the nameplate has a black background instead of red and some of the brightwork has been painted over but she is well cleaned in detail. The stoker looks like Charlie Sinden so the driver may well be Bill Bailey, 'the man-killer', in which case Charlie will not be sitting down for long as the train is passing Shortlands Junction and will soon attack the 1 in 95 up to Bickley Junction and the long drag round Petts Wood and onto Knockholt. Photograph R.C. Riley, The Transport Treasury.

WILLIAM SHAKESPEARE at The Lane on 15 September 1957. The 1935 coaling plant dominates; it rarely let us down but was stopped for overhaul from time to time whereupon Messrs Greenham's Ruston-Bucyrus digger would take up its position 'down the Greenyard', the area of land between the coal road and the turntable, the far side of the bridges. Chief Running Foreman Fred Pankhurst loved this sort of challenge and we always asked for Gerry Compton, their fastest digger-driver. Mac Grant was the Greenham boss we dealt with and he always did us proud. The bridge carries the South London line of the old LB&SCR over The Lane from Battersea Park to Wandsworth Road: the South London was electrified in 1909 with overhead distribution at 3000 Volts AC. Photograph R.C. Riley, The Transport Treasury.

nor drew the fire up to the tubeplate. Indeed the Brits made the noise and the Bulleids burned the coal! The Melesco multiple valve regulator had been tried out on five Eastern A2s and was used on the 7MTs. It gave no trouble nor did we have trouble with slipping when starting provided the driver pulled the reverser back after three or four revolutions to about 30% cut-off – even 25% – whereupon the regulator became a much more sensitive instrument, could be handled with ease and then opened wide as soon as possible. They were rarely if ever short of steam and were light on coal, water and oil although, unlike a Bulleid, a 7MT was a poor tool with low steam pressure for the blower was little use in rallying the boiler. We had some trouble now and again with cylinder and steam chest lubrication so that piston and valve rings suffered to the point of breaking and likewise piston gland lubrication. Boilers gave us no trouble, heated axleboxes were unknown and both engines ran from

The up Golden Arrow passing Shakespeare Halt with a clear chimney top despite the long gradient to Sandwich. The fireman on 70004 in August 1957 could be leaving his fire of Welsh briquettes off the Folkestone Junction stage to get truly hot before getting down to seriously hard work. Photograph R.C. Riley, The Transport Treasury.

A three quarter view of 70014 on 27 October 1957 which shows the lines of a Britannia to perfection. For many years Hampton's Depository provided a marvellous backdrop to photographs taken at Stewarts Lane. The fire is made up for a good start up Grosvenor Road bank but there will be neither smoke nor blowing off over at Victoria. There are more cleaners now the summer is over and she has been well cleaned although the brightwork is now confined to a very short black backed nameplate. Syd Norman, Shop Officeman, has placed a particularly smart pair of flags on the buffer beam for the benefit of the photographer. Photograph R.C. Riley, The Transport Treasury.

10-12 days between the X day examinations although this was supposed to take place on a 6-8 day basis. But at an X day, the repairs and especially the cleaning of tubes and boilers had to be done very thoroughly. The Britannias tended to ride hard but very steadily and the cabs were draughty in cold weather. Battersea had not mastered this little problem although I cannot remember much by way of complaint. Our old men in the top link simply wrapped up but the Stratford men, in their early fifties, rammed a disc board down the back of their seat to deflect the cold air elsewhere and most of them wore Milletts surplus army jerkins over their overalls.

Our engines went to Crewe for intermediate and general repairs and the Works made a very fair job of the overhaul. When 70004 went for an intermediate repair, we asked that special attention be given to all polished brass, steel and copper work. Needless to say nothing was done nor was the engine repainted nor, thank goodness, was the brass and copper painted over but when we started to get repair cards from Carlisle, Holyhead, Edge Hill, Willesden and Camden, we feared the worst. Driver Fred Morley went over to Willesden to bring her home after she had been swanning up and down the West Coast for at least a fortnight and there were no tools of any sort whilst the engine and particularly the cab was filthy. I was so disgusted that I wrote to my Chief (who actually got an apology out of the LM Region) in moderately violent terms. But very quickly she was back on form and Crewe Works had done a good half-sole and healing intermediate repair.

I cannot recall ever 'waiting material' for either engine which speaks well of the liaison between the Southern Region and Crewe Works. We had the benefit of one bay of the old LCDR Longhedge Works in which various machine tools were installed as well as the blacksmith, coppersmith, tinsmith and sheet metal worker which provided an excellent back-up for any extensive shed repair. We had an outstanding Stores Clerk, Bert Freeman, who was just across the way from the Foreman Fitter. Their liaison was excellent and the Waterloo Stores set-up was efficient and simple under a Mr Bill Flutter. I never met the gentleman but spoke to him on several occasions, always to thank him for what he had done for us beyond the call of duty. However neither Mr Flutter nor anybody else outside the Lane could deal with the headlight jinx that hit us during the winter of 1952-53.

Night after night, 70004 with the up Arrow was being stopped for headlamps out when in full flight at Headcorn or Staplehurst. By the time the train had been called forward from the home signal, the driver advised and the fireman sent out in front with a box of matches, far too much time had been lost, a very serious matter indeed on the Southern Region. So far as we could find, nothing like this was happening on other Regions so after a thorough check of a number of headlamps in the Stores, we tried fixing pads on which the lamps rested to eliminate vibration. There was no improvement until Horace King, our Foreman Fitter came to the conclusion that there must be some form of down-draught so we put the lamps on the smokebox side lamp-irons, tucked away inside the deflectors which did the trick. But the engine was now carrying a Victoria via Bexley Heath and Nunhead headcode and we couldn't leave it at that. So Horace came up with those long lamp-irons and we had no more trouble. We never got authority from the CM&EE nor the Motive Power Supt. to alter the design: we simply eliminated (without knowing the reason) a succession of serious delays to our most prestigious train.

We had two grand engines on which it was a pleasure to work. If old Joe Brewer offered me the regulator at Victoria ('take 'er down, Guv') I was a happy man. 70004 would claw her way up the 1 in 64 to Grosvenor Road bridge on about 50% cut-off and roar off across the endless viaducts and bridges of South London, swinging through Herne

Hill and up to Sydenham Hill, no respite until Knockholt was passed. After flying down to Tonbridge at over 80 we would pass through the station at 50 mph and old Joe would shout 'Put 'er on forty Guv'. She would stand this treatment although I used to shorten the cut-off bit by bit when Joe wasn't looking to ease the stoker's lot. I used to fire for Joe on the return and he was merciless, sitting there rocking back and forth on his seat as if to urge his steed even faster over the 'straight' across from Ashford to Tonbridge. I could always keep up with Joe on 70004 but once or twice on a Battle of Britain he nearly had me on my knees!

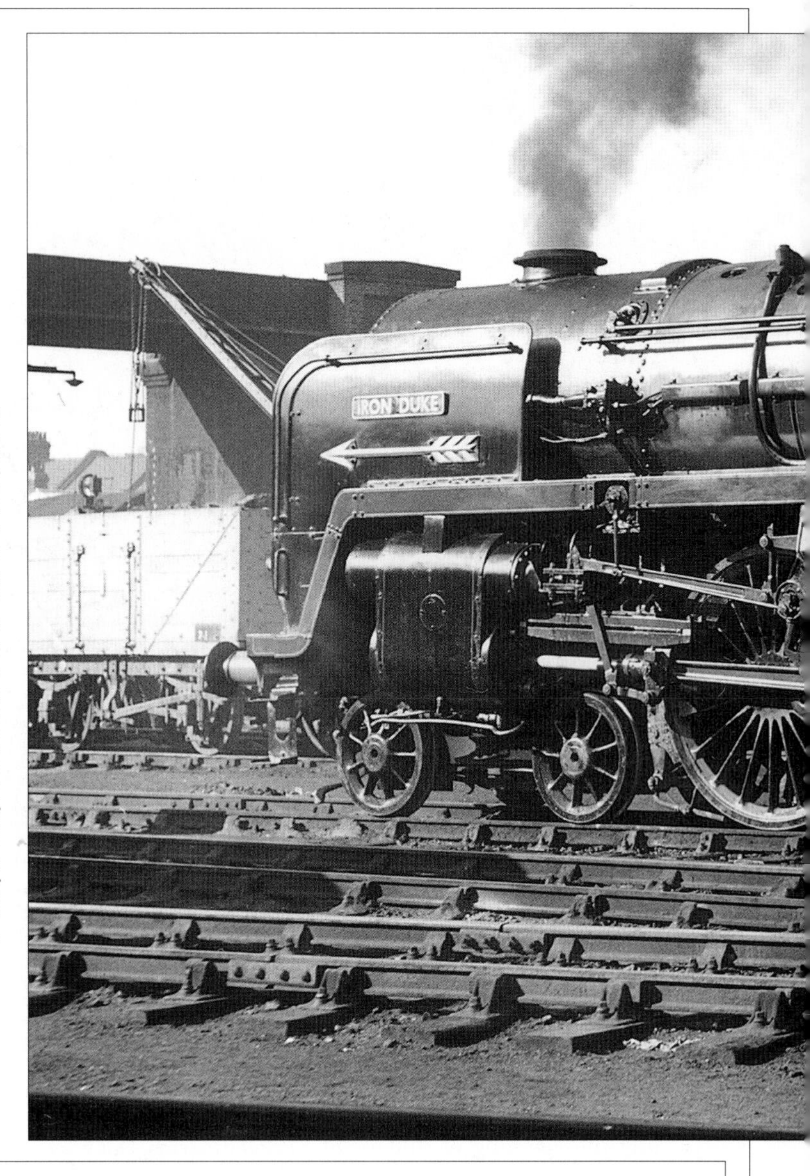

Right. **Driver Charlie Stewart, known as 'Rasher', with his shirt open to the navel and his chest red raw looks down from 70014 IRON DUKE on 20 October 1957. Rasher had an unlimited flow of invective if provoked and, in his prime, had been a fighting man. If one had to 'do' Rasher, one had to be very quiet about it and come to the point before he got wound up. He was a very tough old man but had a heart of gold. After he retired he took over the lavatory and washplace on the Central side at Victoria downstairs alongside the barber's shop to which I went for many years after leaving the Lane. One could hear Rasher leading off at somebody whose aim was not all it should be after which he would come and stand by my chair and entertain Mr Nerwich (the barber) and myself in a loud voice with Battersea banter about the 'old days' much to the amazement and amusement of the other customers. 70014 has been round for coal and is ready to go across to Stew Lane Yard to be attached in rear of the Pullman empties. The jib of old Smithy's ashloading crane can be seen as well as wagons of coal waiting to go up the 'Hopper'. Photograph R.C. Riley, The Transport Treasury.**

Richard Riley made a morning of it and nipped over to Herne Hill after Rasher had left for Victoria. Here is 70014 with a 'boy's' train of only seven Pullmans; there is no non-Pullman stock and it is really a doddle for so powerful an engine. The Fireman may be at work but there is little sign of smoke or steam, a good indication of high superheat and a perfect fire. She is about to face the 1 in 101 up to Sydenham Hill and the roads across to Loughborough Junction and Holborn Viaduct can be seen diverging under the third Pullman. Photograph R.C. Riley, The Transport Treasury.

On 26 May 1958, 70004 has but a few days before she leaves the Lane and goes across to Kentish Town along with 70014. No more will the inmates of that old peoples ward at the hospital south of Orpington hear that lovely whistle blown for their benefit as the Arrow goes by. Both were good engines and they were to do some brilliant high speed work on the Midland main line. Here she is dropping down to Factory Junction and a breath of steam will take her across the viaduct above the shed outlet, onto Grosvenor Road bridge and down into Victoria. On the right is Wandsworth Road station on the South London line facing towards Peckham Rye and London Bridge. Behind the up platform and end-on is the Yardmaster's house. The lines in the foreground lead to Clapham Junction and points south and south-west as well as to Kensington, the North Pole, Willesden, Old Oak, Neasden, Stratford and all points of the compass bar due south. A fascinating piece of railway was the West London on which freight train punctuality was terrible, as the timetable was based on the calendar rather than the clock. But it was an immensely useful and historical artery which served so many of the pre-group railways. Photograph R.C. Riley, The Transport Treasury.

The photograph is dated 17 May 1958 but I have reason to think that it was taken some two years earlier – though I may be wrong. But what a picture of two boys now in their fifties! I know not who they are or who took the photograph but I do hope that they will see themselves and let the Editor know how the picture came about, when it was taken and who were the driver and fireman who absented themselves so kindly in the interests of posterity. Victoria Platform 8 of course. Photograph The Transport Treasury.

27 February 1957. Stewarts Lane, and 70014 prior to working the Golden Arrow. Driver Bill Johnson in No.4 spare link and Fireman Mike Gilbert who after several moves retired from Clacton as a driver; he must have been doing his National Service during my time as I never met him until a few years ago at Clacton. On the ground I am defeated by the gent in the middle and so is everybody else so far, while the two foremen are Bert Humphreys and Lionel King. Both came from elsewhere and had only recently been appointed when the photograph was taken. Photograph R.C. Riley, The Transport Treasury.

'The Shakespeare' ready to leave Stew Lane on a quiet winter Sunday late in 1953. It will be about 12.30 and in five minutes they will be on their way to Victoria for the 'Arrow', duty 4. The cleaners have done a good job and Bill Thorburn, the chargehand, has scoured the buffers and what a difference that inch band round the circumference makes to a flat surface: it was his trademark. One small point used to irritate me on these engines. Sediment in the steam dribbling from the open snifting valves above the cylinders would mark the paintwork almost as soon as it was cleaned and the vertical marks can be clearly seen on the left-hand cylinder casing. Driver Fred Skelly stands by the column. He came up from Plymouth Friary for a driving job before the war but had not lost his soft Devonian way of speech. His stoker on the tender top is Syd Hudson who fired 34088 on the Royal train in October 1954 when the Emperor Haile Selassie of Abysinia came up to London from Portsmouth to be received by the Queen. Both men were a credit to their calling. Photograph Robin Russell.

The Big Tanks

Four of the Standards were but LMS designs modified to take BR details. These were the Ivatt Class 4 Mogul and the Class 2 2-6-0/2-6-2T along with the Fairburn 2-6-4T; all four rode and steamed well, were strong in their power class and enjoyed wide availability. Moreover, all had been running on other Regions and were widely acceptable. The BR Class 4 2-6-4T was the only one of the four to depart in any radical way from the looks of the LMS 'base' design, for in order to fit the required 'universal' L_1 loading gauge the BR version got modified cylinders, a higher pressure boiler and an entirely altered shape. It was 'compacted' as it were, giving it a wholly different, and rather more muscular look. In Scotland they fitted in effortlessly on the sort of duty shown here, the 2.30pm St Enoch-Largs, at Ardrossan behind 80000 (with ex-G&SWR coaches leading) on 12 June 1954. Photograph J.L. Stevenson, courtesy Hamish Stevenson.

80006, sparklingly clean and smooth-lined, at Polmadie on 28 March 1953. Photograph J. Robertson, The Transport Treasury.

80020, Brighton-built and the first one to reach Scotland, carrying the old Caledonian-style 'semaphore' route indicator on the buffer beam, at Edinburgh Princes Street. The big new 2-6-4Ts were seen principally as a shot in the arm for commuter working and were properly targeted (rather than the 'dribs and drabs' approach employed with some other classes) at chosen centres. Scotland and the Southern thus got numbers of them for the best work out of London, Glasgow and Edinburgh and both Regions were rich in lighter work during the day. This might mean a two coach branch shuttle in Sussex or a colliery trip in Renfrewshire. Photograph J. Patterson, The Transport Treasury.

80026 in a perfect portrait, at Dalry Road shed, Edinburgh, a year or two after its arrival in Scotland (at Polmadie) at the end of 1951. Photograph W. Hermiston, The Transport Treasury.

In an almost preservation era state of cleanliness, 80027 is posed with its crew at Polmadie about 1952. In this period it was not at all unusual to see the Scottish Class 4 tanks in this sort of exquisite condition (look at the one behind for instance). The 2-6-4Ts did not appear in number order; 80000 appeared from Derby in September 1952 more than a year after the first one, 80010, was turned out from Brighton. Brighton had in fact reached 80046 by the time 80000 went to Scotland. Photograph J. Robertson, The Transport Treasury.

Kentish Town in the rain, July 1953. 80060 was one of several (another is inside the roundhouse) which went to Bedford and Kentish Town new in 1952. These were 80044-80048, followed by another five (that magic number again) early the following year, 80059-80063. 80060 was a Bedford engine; once Midland crews got used to them they did well on top link St Pancras-Bedford trains as well as (the Standard principle at work again) minor duties in between. They were heavier on water than the native LM 2-6-4Ts (the opposite was claimed on the Southern!) but admired for good steaming and free running. Timekeeping was excellent, but all left the Midland line sheds in 1955-56. Photograph J. Patterson, The Transport Treasury.

80000
To traffic 26/9/52
SHEDS
Ayr 9/52
Corkerhill 11/52
Hurlford 25/9/61
Corkerhill 1/1/62
Ardrossan 1/10/62
Corkerhill 15/6/64
REPAIRS
24/11/54-14/12/54**LI** St.Rollox
24/8/57-19/9/**57HG** St Rollox
19/9/58-23/10/58**LC** Cowlairs
30/7/60-9/9/60**LI** Cowlairs
10/9/63-12/10/**63HG** Cowlairs
Withdrawn 12/66; stored Corkerhill 8/66-3/67
Cut up Shipbreaking Industries, Faslane, 4/67

Left. The other great area of operation of the 2-6-4Ts was the LT&S, on the heavy commuter work out of Fenchurch Street. Bolstering the ailing Stanier three cylinder 2-6-4Ts (the LT was notoriously short of fitting staff) they kept the service going (just) until electrification. 80103, serving to demonstrate the application of water treatment briquettes at Plaistow in the 1950s, has an odd distinction, first highlighted by P. Atkins in British Railways Illustrated in August 1996, *The First One To Go.* It was indeed the first Standard withdrawn, with a terrible fracture to the frame. Its storage due to this defect (it could hardly be moved, such was the state it was in) began in January 1962 while the final long-stored Crosti conversion, 92022, did not come out of Crewe until July that year. This meant, curiously, that the 999 Standards were never operational (works visits aside) at the same time. Now who could have predicted that?

Below. 80032 on the Southern Region, at Eastleigh shed on 7 August 1960. Brighton built 120 of the BR Class 4 tanks, and over half of these actually ended up working on the Region, including those LMR ones swopped at the end of the 1950s for Fairburn versions, to resentment that can still be found among Bletchley and Watford men even today. Photograph W. Hermiston, The Transport Treasury.

The Class 3 Tanks

A Class 3 tank in the north of England. 82029 (at Kirkby Stephen East on 7 July 1956) was the last of the class, one of just four allocated to the NER. This was odd, given that the new types should have been concentrated so far as was possible. The rest went to the WR and the SR and 82026-82029 should really perhaps have gone with them. They found work enough alongside the smaller Standard and Ivatt Moguls but with work disappearing they finally came south towards the end of 1963, to Guildford and Bournemouth; as far from Stainmore as might be imagined – in every respect. In a further change of scene, all four ended up at Nine Elms, working the Waterloo-Clapham ECS trains. Photograph A.G. Ellis, The Transport Treasury.

82024, an Exmouth Junction engine, on duty at Exeter St Davids on 31 July 1955. All three engines on these pages ended up at Nine Elms. Photograph J. Robertson, The Transport Treasury.

82010 makes a blasting show of it at Exmouth Junction on 13 August 1954. This is the same location seen in the 82000 section of the earlier 'Book of the BR Standards'; beyond the tunnel, westwards, is Exeter Central and, beyond that, St Davids while out of sight to the right lies the Exmouth Junction concrete depot and engine shed. Photograph J. Robertson, The Transport Treasury.

70002 GEOFFREY CHAUCER, at Doncaster shed before re-roofing, on 14 June 1958. This illustrates well the original batch of engines, with the modified smoke deflectors following the WR Milton accident in 1955, in which the drivers' sighting of signals being obscured by the earlier handrails was cited as a likely cause. The engine is fresh out of the nearby works after a Classified Repair and repaint, and has the then new BR lion and wheel crest. Notice the notorious flexible screen hanging out between the engine cab and the 'inset' tender, the easy access afforded to the pipe work on the side of the firebox and the position of the exhaust injector just in front of the trailing truck – on LMS engines this item of equipment was under the footplate and most inaccessible. Photograph J. Robertson, The Transport Treasury.

MAINTAINING STANDARDS

Notes by Allan C Baker

Over the years much criticism has been levelled regarding the decision in 1948 by the newly constituted British Transport Commission, and its subsidiary body the Railway Executive, to design and built a series of 'standard' steam locomotives for service on the lines of the four constituent railway companies. Whatever the rights and wrongs of this decision, it is usually blamed by those same critics on the 'engineers', led by Robin Riddles who had been appointed Board Member for Mechanical & Electrical Engineering, within the Executive. Riddles was an LMS man through and through, and before that LNWR, and had latterly been a Vice President of the LMS. Quite naturally therefore, he surrounded himself at his headquarters with former colleagues from that railway company, and the locomotives they designed embodied more of the practices of the LMS then any other design school. But it has to be remembered that, then as now, the 'engineers' only provided designs to meet the needs of the 'operators'. It was the Motive Power Department in the new organisation that was responsible for running the railway; it dictated the locomotive needs and this too, was headed by a thoroughgoing LMS man, the redoubtable Colonel Harold Rudgard.

Both Riddles and Rudgard were extremely strong willed men, used to getting there own way and, therefore, despite pressure to appoint men to his 'top team' from companies other then the LMS, Riddles chose as his principal assistants Roland C. Bond to take charge of locomotive construction and maintenance and E. Stewart Cox similarly to take charge of design. The scene therefore, was firmly set, and the 'operators' had agreed a need for additional motive power covering all power ranges. However, in a desire to break down some of the obvious Regional barriers, a series of 'standard' locomotives was to be designed and built for use across all the newly formed regions, which to a large extent corresponded to the old company geographical boundaries.

Whatever the rights and wrongs of this action, of one thing there is, to my mind, absolutely no doubt that Cox and his team put enormous effort in attempts to lessen the work load of those whose daily chore was to drive, service and maintain the new locomotives. One has only to read Cox's writings, so ably summarised in his book *British Railways Standard Steam Locomotives* (Ian Allan 1966) to appreciate this. That in all cases these ideals were not wholly delivered was not for the want of trying, and in my experience so far as the servicing and maintenance of the locomotives they were largely successful. It was unfortunate that it was with the footplatemen themselves that in so many cases these efforts fell on stony ground. This was never more so than on the erstwhile Great Western Railway, where the Britannia Pacifics went down so badly with the West Country men. It was not until all that Region's allocation was concentrated at Cardiff Canton that anything approaching the best was got out of

A lovely view of Stratford's Driver A. Bird, checking the oil level in the mechanical lubricator on the right-hand foot framing of a Britannia at Stratford on 6 April 1961. Although lubricators were filled by servicing staff, the driver was called on to check the oil level as a part of his preparation duties. These lubricators had a sight glass to show the oil level; it can just be seen, but they were not to be relied upon. Observe that lovely chime whistle – the operating cord ran through the hollow handrail. Cox is on record as saying that they wanted these new engines to sound different. They certainly did and the note, I felt, was deeper than the A4s.

Haymarket shed in Edinburgh, on 10 March 1956. The engine is Standard Class 5 73105, one of a batch allocated from new to the Scottish Region, in this case to Eastfield in Glasgow. 73105-73109 all went there new between December 1955 and January 1956. The driver (unfortunately we know not his name) is obviously going about his preparation duties; note that for this class of engine, like most of the Standards, he would not need a pit – a great advantage of these engines. Observe the row of grease nipples under the cylinder drain cock gear; these would feed the bogie suspension arrangements through a series of pipes. The projection on the front of the cylinder cover is the pressure relief valve; this would relieve any excessive pressure or water trapped in the cylinder. On the top of the steam chest is the anti-vacuum valve, which allowed both ends of the cylinder to be connected together when the engine was coasting, thus preventing a vacuum being created and ashes etc, being drawn into the valve chest and cylinder from the smokebox. The device on the side of the smokebox is the large and small vacuum ejector, for creating the brake vacuum. Photograph J. Robertson, The Transport Treasury.

them. As is well known, the same engines were a Godsend to the authorities and men on the former Great Eastern section of the Eastern Region, but in this case they displaced designs underpowered for the job to be done, the LNER Gresley Sandringham 4-6-0s, which had acquired a rather unenviable reputation. This case was far removed from the much-liked and celebrated GW Castles on which the

Another of the Class 5 engines new to Eastfield, 73107, inside the Repair Shop at Perth on 20 May 1964, by which time it had been reallocated to that shed – although it was transferred to Motherwell the following month. Perth had one of a number of what were called 'Outstation Repair Shops', introduced by the LMS. Their workloads were controlled centrally, and not by the Motive Power Districts in which they were situated. They were in effect outstations of the Main Works, and assisted in the lighter Classified, and more particularly, Unclassified repairs. Others were at Polmadie, Carlisle and Rugby for example. We know not what 73107 was in for on this occasion, but it does not look as if work has yet started. Photograph R.F. Smith, The Transport Treasury.

Western men had been brought up, and which were so completely master of the job. That the Western men were accustomed to driving on the right-hand side of the cab, and route signal sighting was designed around this, and that the new locomotives all had left-hand drive, seemed to go unnoticed in the Colonel's office!

Insofar as labour saving devices in the preparation and disposal of steam locomotives were concerned, it could be argued that the GWR was the furthest behind. Drop or rocking grates, hopper ashpans and self cleaning smoke boxes had been introduced to some sort of extent by all the other three companies, but it was perhaps on the LMS that such developments had made the most significant inroads. Roller bearing axle boxes had been introduced too, though the Swindon designed coupled wheel axle box arrangement as further developed by Stanier when he arrived on the LMS, if properly maintained, had almost eliminated the incidence of hot axle bearings. So, Cox and his team were faced with the job of designing locomotives to embody both the latest developments from the LMS, but at the same time ensuring that innovative and proven good practice from the other three constituents were not ignored. To help with this the detail design work was spread around various Regional drawing offices, of all four pre-1948 companies. Close overall control by the HQ team, however, ensured that by and large, LMS ideas prevailed. Partly, but not wholly born out of available capacity, production of the new locomotives, of which there were finally no less than 999, was spread around the workshops of all the former Big Four companies.

It cannot be doubted that the work done in equipping the locomotives with the devices mentioned above greatly lightened the load of the shed based servicing staff. Smokeboxes no longer had to be daily emptied by hand, and fires no longer had to be drawn out through the firehole door with long and difficult to manoeuvre shovels. Similarly, the hopper ashpans were designed to empty themselves directly into the ash pits. On the road, rocking grates enabled the crew to break up clinker without the need to resort to similarly unwieldy long and heavy darts, and other implements. Lubrication of most of the joints and bearings that formerly required attention by the driver on preparation, used soft grease lubrication, and these only had to be attended to on the 'X' day examinations and then by maintenance staff. Thus, with no inside motion to attend too, and if the engine had roller bearings throughout, the driver only had the side and connecting rod bearings to worry about on his preparation. Much else was done to ease the lot of maintenance staff; the sort of items that would need attention were much more accessible, and not hidden away in inaccessible corners of the cab. To give one example, the main steam take-off for the cab controls, injectors, vacuum ejector, brakes and so on was located outside the cab and on top of the firebox, so that any attention to it was very easy. You did not have to crawl up into the upper reaches of the cab roof and stand, precariously perched, on the cab

Left. **The cleanest engine in Wigan, perhaps, on 1 June 1962 when the picture was taken at 78063's home shed of Wigan ex-L&Y. The Standard Class 2 tender engine had been new here in November 1956, and remained until transferred to Willesden in May 1963. She would appear to be recently ex-works and along with all other members of this 65 strong class had been built at Darlington, which along with ten of the small Class 2 2-6-2 tanks were the only Standards built there. The Class 2 2-6-0s did not have the cab cantilevered out from the engine, and thus had a conventional footplate with fall plate between engine and tender, the only 'Standard' engines to exhibit this feature. Apart from placing a number of components outside the cab, and generally making others more accessible, these engines differed little from their Ivatt LMS predecessors; note for example the lubricator atomisers each side of the smokebox, and the vacuum ejector alongside the smokebox. Doesn't she catch the sun nicely! Photograph The Transport Treasury.**

controls in a most uncomfortable way, to repack glands and the like. Like many steam jobs, it would barely be legal today! Some of the ideals, I have to say, appear to have gone out of the window with the smaller designs, several of which were but marginally updated versions of latter-day Ivatt LMS designs. Interestingly it was some of these, the Class 3 2-6-2T and the Class 2-6-0 tender engines, that appear to have found the most favour on the Western Region!

My personal experiences of 'maintaining Standards' were confined to but a few classes. At Crewe North in my time we only had Britannias, the solitary Class 8 Pacific No.71000, and a couple of the class 2 tender engines. As visitors we often saw the Class 5 4-6-0s, and the Class 4 2-6-4Ts and later when I had periods at Crewe South we used to get the 9F 2-10-0s visiting. Oh, and the occasional Clan Pacific visited Crewe North, and of course, any passenger or mixed traffic engine repaired in Crewe Works would spend a little time with us 'running in'. We had little to do with these for if any problems arose they would be attended to by 'Works' staff, and we had a resident 'Works' fitter at the shed for this purpose. Such engines would almost always have returned 'home' before their first 'X' day examination was due.

The use of two cylinders – the three cylinder No.71000 aside – made performing valve and piston examinations a much more simple operation than on our other Class 7 engines, all of which had three cylinders. The periodicity for valve and piston examinations was longer too, for example the BR Pacifics had what we called a 'No.8 V&P', the largest such examination undertaken at the sheds, at between 40,000 and 48,000 miles, while similar work on most of the LMS Class 7 engines was performed at lesser intervals of between 30,000 and 36,000 miles, so the job came around more often. Another bonus on those engines with a leading bogie was the use of the LNER three bar slide bar arrangement as it was possible to get the piston out of the front of the cylinder without splitting the piston rod to crosshead taper joint. As removing the taper cotter, and splitting the taper interface were among the most arduous jobs in motion work, if the crosshead itself did not need re-metalling this was welcomed by us all. The smaller classes with a leading truck rather than a bogie however, had the LMS arrangement of twin bars, one at the top and one at the bottom of the crosshead, to maintain the front cylinder overthrow on curves to keep within the required loading gauge.

Above. **I cannot ever recall a Britannia suffering from a hot axle box, but it would seem that this fate has befallen 70044, seen here at Carlisle Upperby on 7 August 1965. This engine is one of those fitted with plain bearing axle boxes on the coupled wheels and trailing truck, and I suspect falling maintenance standards in these latter days were the cause of the particular axle journal running warm. The intermediate coupled wheels have been removed on the Upperby wheel drop and then 70044 has been moved out of the way while they receive attention; perhaps they had to be sent to Crewe Works for repairs, although it would have been possible to true up the journals on the shed lathe. There is some form of hoist in the background but I doubt this would have had the capacity to lift such a large locomotive as this. Along with the other Pacifics the Britannias had smokebox mounted 'Melesco' multiple valve regulators, fitted on the dry side of the superheater header; notice the external rodding via the crank alongside the dome. It was reckoned to give the drivers better control during slipping but they were a pain to maintain once they had started to 'blow through'. Note the lack of flexible screen between cab and tender, doubtless removed by exasperated maintenance staff; the live steam injector is to be seen in front of the trailing truck, the latter with its plain bearing axle box. The small valve complete with operating rod just under the foot framing and alongside the firebox is the operating valve connected to the driver's control lever, for the steam operated cylinder drain cock gear. This was another labour saving device for the driver, and it has to be said caused us little effort so far as maintenance was concerned. Photograph R.F. Smith, The Transport Treasury.**

Steam locomotives in my experience always seemed to get through a lot of coupled wheel springs and we always seemed to be changing those of the laminated variety due to broken leafs. I do not feel as if the Britannias were any better than other classes, but they were much easier to change. There were no adjustable hangers, instead there was a neat system of cotters at each end of the rectangular hangers, so that it was only necessary to take the weight by jacking the engine up to remove the cotters. With the screw thread arrangement of the older engines it was necessary to run the nuts up and down, frequently having to contend with partially seized threads. A resort to extra long spanners, extension tubes and so on was then necessary, and in

Right and below. **Two of the shed's allocation of 9F 2-10-0s, inside the Repair Shed at York on 2 May 1964. The one with the smokebox door open is 92211, and both locomotives are undergoing a level of valve and piston examinations. Notice the piston valves (the dumbbell-like objects) and pistons laying around on the shed floor (one piston valve is in the vice) and the multiple ring heads – six rings on each valve head. So far as valve and piston examinations were concerned, freight engines were not maintained as assiduously as their passenger or mixed traffic counterparts, and items were attended to when 'booked', as opposed to a pre-set mileage interval. This is doubtless why neither 2-10-0 has the motion dropped for attention at the same time. Only the valves and pistons have been removed – the motion would only be attended to at the same time if it had either been 'booked' by the driver, or found wanting attention by the maintenance staff. Engines used on higher speed duties had this work done on a mileage basis, irrespective of condition. On the front of 92205 and under the smokebox door can be seen the pressure relief valves removed from the cylinder covers, and 92211 seems to have had its self cleaning smokebox arrangements removed. This locomotive is fitted with AWS; note the protection bracket for the receiver by the screw coupling, while its sister is not so fitted. Photographs R.F. Smith, The Transport Treasury.**

those small shallow and dirty pits that were the norm of steam motive power depots. It was not unknown either, to enlist the help of the Blacksmith with his torch to heat up the offending nuts, or in extreme cases cut them off completely, but this was a practice frowned on from above, far better to

Left, right and below right. **Three views of 70040, CLIVE of INDIA, outside the Jubilee shed at Stratford on 2 November 1960. A Norwich engine at the time, she was transferred to Immingham the following month. We have here a very nice close up of the trailing truck, and this is one of the engines with plain bearing axle boxes – note the additional oil reservoir and feeder pipe. This extra lubrication arrangement was added after some early problems with this design of box. It became heated due, it was said, to its close proximity to the firebox. Again the ease of access to the various pipes and valves will be noted, along with the exhaust injector – the truck by the way, was based on Bulleid's design for his Pacifics, so a little bit of Southern practice crept in here. The large valve on the firebox above the injector is the blowdown cock, but notice it is threaded to take the washout water inlet pipe, as these engines could be washed out with hot water where such facilities existed at the sheds. This allowed quicker turn round times as it was not necessary to completely cool down the boilers, as was the case prior to washing out with cold water. Note the engine retains the LNER squared boss and bolt fixing of the return arm; most engines later had this replaced by the spigot and four stud LMS arrangement, as the former was prone to fracturing of the arm itself. AWS battery box on framing and modified smoke deflectors will also be observed. Photographs R.F. Smith, The Transport Treasury.**

let us sweat! Incidentally, the later BR-built LMS design Class 5s, also had the cotter arrangement rather than screws and nuts.

So why were many of the classes so unpopular with the crews? one asks ones self. Much was liked and I never found an engineman who did not appreciate the arrangement of the cab on the tender engines where the footplate was cantilevered out from the locomotive with the result that there was no traditional fall plate between engine and tender (the sole exception to this was the Class 2 2-6-0, which had a conventional arrangement). This made firing conditions much better, with no moving floor underfoot. But the BR arrangement, when combined with a high tender front plate, tended to introduce draughts into the cab, and these in turn tended to pick up coal dust and made for a much more dirty and dusty environment. On the earlier Britannias and the Clans with 'inset' tenders a flexible screen was introduced between cab and tender to counteract this, and while partially successful it required a lot of maintenance and often fell into disrepair. I recall that, well after large numbers of the class started to be allocated to Crewe North in 1961-63, perennial complaints by crews of draughts and resultant dust – they often came off the engines looking dirtier than we did after spending the day in a smokebox removing superheater elements! Complaints got to epidemic levels and something had to be done – Footplate Inspectors went out to look see, and came back as dirty as the crews! Much effort was put into maintaining the neglected screens and some improvements ensued. After much difficulty by our stores people a limited supply of new screens were acquired, and one or two different materials and fastening arrangements were tried in attempts to make them last longer. But the problem remained and one has only to look at photographs of the engines in service to see evidence of poorly fitting screens, hanging out between engine and tender. The later engines with the high-sided tenders had a different arrangement, and they never seemed to suffer quite as badly from draughts. As a result they never had screens fitted.

Because (as indicated earlier) the Swindon-Stanier plain bearing axle box had been developed to deliver such high reliability, the cost of fitting roller bearings was questioned. Hence, some of the Britannias had plain boxes on all their coupled wheels while others had roller bearings only on the driving axles; plain bearing on the trailing truck were also a feature of some members of the class. All, however, had roller bearings on the bogie and tenders. Roller bearings of course, gave maintenance staff an additional job as we had to fill them with grease at the 7-9 week examinations, a boring job sitting underneath engines pumping two guns full of grease into each box. But we used to cheat on the truck and tender, by taking the outside covers off and packing the bearings by hand! Another job that helped the servicing staff but not us, was the self cleaning smokeboxes, as we were the ones who had to remove the screens

and other impedimenta, so as to get access to all the other equipment. Of course, everything in a smokebox is dirty, dry dirt rather than oily dirt, and it used to penetrate to our most personal quarters – and there were no showers at sheds in those days!

It was of course, not only shed maintenance staff and practices that Cox and his team had in mind in the designs. The locomotives were intended to cover greater mileages between Classified Repairs, and to require less work when they were due for attention. For example, the horn guides were welded into the frames and embraced the entire horn gap in the frame plates. They were so designed to strengthen this otherwise vulnerable part of the main frame, and reduce the incidence of fracturing emanating from the top corners. These horn guides were also mounted central to the longitudinal centre line of the frame plates themselves, thus better distributing the traction load paths between axle box and main frame. This method of frame construction had first been introduced in this country by Bulleid on his Merchant Navy and West Country Pacifics. Hitherto, except in Bulleid's case, practice generally had been to mount the guides flush with the inside of the frame plate. By this redesign, the frame plates themselves were, of course, closer together, making the distance between the wheels and the frames larger. As a result of these, and other ideas, the engines did generally achieve longer mileages between repairs, and the costs of such repairs were less then their more conventional brethren, but I have to say not by any orders of magnitude. Indeed, while the horn guide arrangement

eliminated fractures in the classic top corners, some of the stresses were transferred to the bottom corners, where the spring hangers were fixed, and fracturing developed in this area.

So what should we make of these engines from a maintenance point of view? Well to my mind enormous and extremely laudable efforts went into making our collective lots better, crews, preparation and disposal staff, and maintenance staff alike. Many crews found fault, despite having for example cab controls much closer to hand. Moreover there was prejudice abroad, and what was seen on some regions as an infiltration of LMS ideas. And as for those draughts and left-hand drive! I doubt however, any maintenance or servicing staff had much to complain about, I certainly did not. And, would not our railway history be the poorer without them!

Top and above. **Stratford on 28 October 1960 with 70009 ALFRED the GREAT of Norwich outside the Jubilee Shed, doubtless waiting its next turn of duty. Notice the roller bearing axle box on the trailing truck and the external mounted steam valves just in front of the cab for the injector and carriage warming apparatus. These valves would have been located inside the cab on pre-nationalisation designs, and as a result not only more difficult to maintain, but a much greater problem for the crews if there was any steam leakage. This engine and 70040 retain the flexible draught screen between the engine and tender, and they look in reasonable nick too. Photographs R.F. Smith, The Transport Treasury.**

70015 at Plymouth Laira in the mid-1950s. APOLLO carries an 81A Old Oak Common shedplate so the period must be between its going to the Western Region in May 1953 and December 1956 when a transfer to Cardiff Canton took place. APOLLO and sister engine 70019 LIGHTNING are standing on a road which seems to be equipped for the discharge of rail tank wagons – notice the pipes in the foreground. This could be a legacy of oil burning after the war, the lagged pipes carrying the heavy oil, pre-heated in the tank wagons so as to assist unloading. Notice the Western Region lamp brackets, which were at right angles to everybody else's! Just discernible is that LIGHTNING has its right front cylinder cover removed; there is an interesting bit of spring on the footstep and some other 'bits' on the framing just above the buffer – both locomotives have had a bump in this area just behind the buffer beam. Photograph J. Robertson, The Transport Treasury.

Setting the valves of a 9F 2-10-0. Notice that only the connecting rod is in place (no side rods). The contraption under the flangeless centre coupled wheel is for turning the driving wheel and hence the crank, so that the Valve Setter can check the valve events and make any necessary adjustments. The turning device is operated by a compressed air engine. That's the air hose in the bloke's hand, while with his other hand he is marking a position on the tyre to be able (as part of the valve setting process) to return the wheelset to the same exact position. Note the method of balance weight on the right-hand wheel, plates fitted to each side and filled with the required amount of lead. The engine is jacked up at the front to lift the wheels just off the rails making movement by the air engine possible. Packing would be inserted between the axle boxes and the horn cross stays, to replicate their 'running' position. This was the standard method of setting valves on steam locomotives in main workshops.

Ivatts In All But Name

84029, the last steam locomotive to be built at Darlington, completed on 11 June 1957; some diesel shunter cabs in primer paint stand in the background. Darlington built diesel locomotives until 1964 – the same year, funnily enough, that 84029 (which had been its 2,269th locomotive) was condemned at Wellingborough, just seven years old.

84019 on Lees shed, Oldham, about 1956; this would one of the engines for the 'Delph Donkey', the push-pull Delph branch train. Photograph Jim Davenport, Initial Photographics.

84008 at Derby on 6 July 1954, during its time as a Burton engine. Seamless extensions of the Ivatt Class 2 fleet, the 84000s were built at Crewe (84000-84019) and Darlington (84020-84029); the Crewe ones went to the LM, mostly in the north-west and the Darlington ones to the Southern. Push-pull fitting began with the three engines working out of Fleetwood. Photograph J. Robertson, The Transport Treasury.

84025 at Ashford, the east end of the up side platform. The Southern's Darlington-built engines all went to Kent; with electrification they went to other parts of the Region – Brighton, Eastleigh and Exmouth Junction – but then a decision was made to transfer all of them to the LMR. All had gone before the year 1961 was out. Photograph Collection Gavin Whitelaw.

The longest-lived BR Standard, Class 7MT 4-6-2 70013 OLIVER CROMWELL (May 1951-August 1968) stands at Colchester on 14 August 1953, still with fifteen years of BR service ahead of it. 70013 has already acquired several modifications, most notably plain section coupling rods following the buckling problems experienced when the class newly entered traffic in 1951. Photograph J. Robertson, The Transport Treasury.

STANDARDS THAT NEVER WERE

By Philip Atkins

In 1948, when the *genre* was first being formulated, it was possible to believe that eventually *thousands* of Standards would monopolise British Railways operations. As it was, despite an intrinsic life expectancy averaging around 40 years apiece, the 999 Standards all came and went within a period of merely 17½ years, and statistically never accounted for more than 22 per cent of the continually declining (from 1950) BR steam locomotive stock. By autumn 1968 it was all over and capital investment equivalent to about £400 million at 2002 price levels had been prematurely written off.

But then nothing ever seemed to go strictly according to plan wherever the BR Standards were concerned, even when the fleet was being built up in the first instance. Thus although no fewer than 740 units had been authorised between November 1949 and February 1952 for construction on the 1951-54 annual building programmes, only 492 had been completed by 31 December 1954 on account of the widespread shortage of steel which was subject to rationing between consumers. To get round this in July 1953 the Railway Executive seriously considered ordering Standards from the private British locomotive building industry, and actually obtained quotations from Robert Stephenson & Hawthorns for fifty Class 5 4-6-0s, and from the North British Locomotive Company and Vulcan Foundry for thirty-five 2-10-0s each. Initially it was proposed to order twenty 2-10-0s and thirty 4-6-0s from contractors for delivery in 1955, but sadly Class 5s bearing hexagonal and 9Fs carrying diamond shaped worksplates were not to be. Then it was subsequently decided not to order any locomotives at all on the 1955 Programme in order to let the earlier programmes catch up. In the end a token thirty, later increased to thirty-five, Class 5 4-6-0s were ordered from BR workshops for 1955.

Almost by way of compensation the 1956 Building Programme, as initially tabulated in February 1955, was to have provided for 384 new Standards. However, there was also an alternative scaled down version ('Plan B') which took into account the 269 engines already outstanding, and the impending major change in traction policy. 'Plan A' would have included more than *fifty* new 4-6-2s, i.e. thirty-six additional Class 7 Britannias, for the LMR, ER, and WR, plus twenty Clans for the *North Eastern* Region. At that moment fifteen Clans, Nos.72010-72024, were still outstanding from the 1954 Programme agreed three years earlier, ten more for the Scottish Region and five for the Southern. Even their prospective names had recently been published, but these were formally cancelled only two months later in April 1955 as one of the opening shots of the *British Railways Modernisation and Re-Equipment Plan*, which had been hastily drafted in late 1954 and made public in January 1955.

The Modernisation Plan as at that time conceived looked forward only fifteen years to 1970 during which, *inter alia*, it envisaged a substantial reduction, but *not* total elimination, of the substantial BR steam locomotive fleet. It was anticipated that then there would perhaps remain around 5,000 steam locomotives of modern design, mainly post-1932 LMS and BR Standard, principally in northern England, plus the Bulleid 4-6-2s then at the beginning of their rebuilding, in the south. By 1970 some 2,500 main line diesel locomotives would be in service, but to determine the design of these it was proposed to order 160 diesel electrics in the 800-2,300HP range, to be divided between the London Midland and Eastern Regions, plus fourteen diesel hydraulics for the

70054 DORNOCH FIRTH was the last British Pacific to be built, in September 1954, although a few months later a further thirty-six Class 7s (and twenty Class 6s) were provisionally indented for on the 1956 Programme, only to be deleted again soon after. Although double chimneys featured on early schemes, about 1949, it was subsequently decided that a well proportioned single exhaust would suffice. Steaming problems with increasingly poor coal in the late 1950s nevertheless nearly prompted the Western Region to equip one of its Britannias with a double blastpipe and chimney. These were already beginning to appear on the 2-10-0s, but by this time every resource was being devoted to dieselisation and the project was shelved. Photograph J. Patterson, The Transport Treasury.

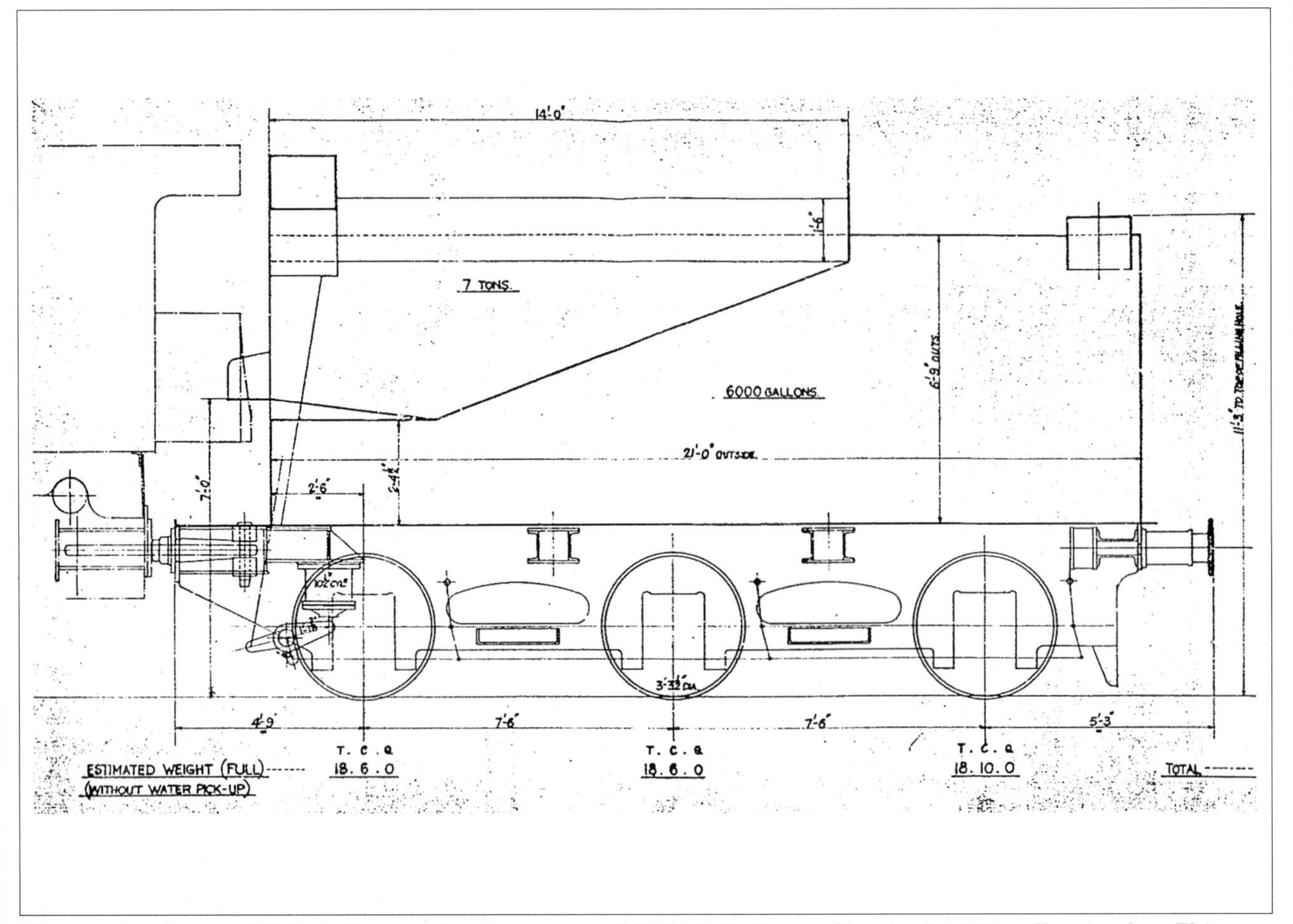

The previously unpublished diagram for the proposed British Railways Standard 6,000 gallon tender. This was designed for attachment to the Class 9F 2-10-0s initially proposed for the Southern Region, which was devoid of water troughs. Derived from the basic BR1 type the wheelbase is 1ft longer to match a corresponding increase in the length of the tender tank, which is also 2½in wider and 9in taller. Courtesy F. James.

Western, which was already characteristically pursuing its own agenda and proposed to eliminate steam working altogether by 1968!

In early 1955 it was proposed that these pilot diesels should be carefully evaluated over a three year period, 1958-1960, *before* any more were ordered. It was also stated that it was intended 'to build no new passenger or suburban steam locomotives after the 1956 programme, and to terminate the building of all steam locomotives within a few years.'

In fact, within a few months it was decided to cancel outright many of the passenger steam locomotives only just proposed, including all fifty-six 4-6-2s and many 2-6-4Ts. In the event, by the time D5500 arrived from Brush Ltd and D8000 from English Electric slightly earlier than originally anticipated in mid-1957, already orders totalling no less than *444* main line diesels, inclusive of the 174 'pilots' had been placed by BR! Furthermore the delivery rate of main line diesels hit a peak in 1961, and diesel traction had already beaten steam into second place on BR by the end of 1962, when in 1955 it was anticipated it would only just be taking off.

Only a few years earlier, in 1952, it had been difficult to make a cogent case for main line dieselisation on British Railways in economically crippled Britain. Then, *four* Class 6 4-6-2s could be built for the cost of one slightly less powerful diesel electric locomotive. Two 1,600HP units had to be used, actually with *excess* potential, to match one Class 8 4-6-2 on the West Coast Main Line, and in certain locations, owing to track circuiting, an extra locomotive unit could necessitate the deduction of one carriage. There could also be train heating problems in winter. Operating costs were very similar, i.e. fuel plus crew wages, but depreciation and interest charges for the expensive diesels were enormous. In the event of full dieselisation, as was currently rapidly taking place in the USA, allegedly with considerable economic benefits, it was estimated that the total cost of oil fuel would be similar to that of the current coal bill. However, this would involve valuable foreign exchange and the fuel itself would have to be procured from the Middle East, which was as volatile in the early 1950s as it would be half a century later. A theoretical costing exercise on the Southern Region made in 1954 showed *total* steam and diesel costs per mile to be almost identical, but at least all the traditional steam facilities were already in place. (This analysis could not take into account, however, the increasingly severe problems of coal procurement and footplate staff recruitment which BR was then experiencing; these were significant factors in the move away from steam traction thereafter).

In November 1956, before the first 'pilot' diesel had even been delivered, the *Progress Report of the Main Line Diesel Locomotive Panel* advocated the procurement of *at least* 4,150 main line diesels plus 1,350 electric locomotives during 1959-65, if indeed BR workshops and private industry could meet this huge demand. This was despite an April 1956 report 'dealing with the rather unsatisfactory performance of the main line diesel locomotives operating on the L M Region', in which 'it was clearly inferred that it was in the interest of the (British Transport) Commission to adhere to the intention of carrying out trials with the locomotives already authorised before placing further large orders'. Considering what later actually happened this same document had the effrontery to contain the following platitude. *'As schemes for the introduction of diesel locomotive traction are, however, required to be economically justified, excessive charges for the obsolescence of steam locomotives prematurely displaced must be avoided, and thus the number of new locomotives built in any year must have some regard to the number of steam locomotives falling due for replacement.'* Strangely the report did not *totally* rule out the

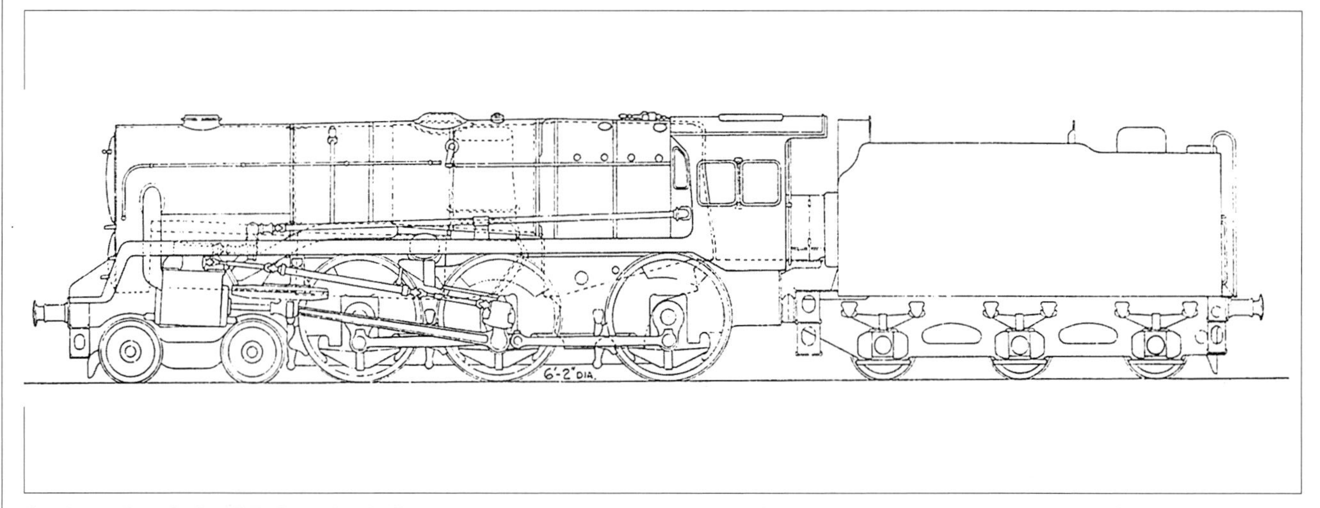

Outline sketch for BR Standard Class 5 4-6-0 provided with both Caprotti poppet valve gear and Crosti boiler. The latter would actually have been developed from the BR4 boiler fitted to the Standard Class 4 4-6-0 and the tender shown is the high capacity BR1F fitted only to 9F 2-10-0s allocated to the ER and Class 5 4-6-0s on the Southern. There is no evidence that this was a serious proposal. The BR Caprotti Class 5s were being designed at Derby just as the Crosti 2-10-0s entered traffic during the summer of 1955.

possibility of further freight and mixed traffic steam locomotives being ordered, but only if '*there was a clear need for new locomotives (which cannot be met otherwise than by building steam locomotives) to maintain or improve services and utilise fitted freight vehicles, pending ultimate electrification or conversion to diesel traction of the services for which the locomotives are required*'.

Even at the time the original 1956 steam programme was outlined, in February 1955, it would seem that it was hoped that it would be the last. Possibly at least partly for reasons of 'image', as indicated earlier the proposed fifty-six new 4-6-2s were quickly deleted. Likewise were thirty of the fifty-four 2-6-4Ts, twenty of them destined for the Western Region on which the 2-6-2T had hitherto reigned supreme. Even the final five which actually were built, Nos.80150-80154, were evidently briefly in abeyance, but were erected as all the parts for them had already been fabricated. However, the order for 101 2-10-0s still stood, and was actually slightly increased as will be seen later. Forty additional Class 4 4-6-0s were deleted, as were thirteen Class 3 2-6-0s, and ten Class 2 and ten Class 3 2-6-2Ts. Three Class

Although only ten Class 6MT Clans were actually built, for the Scottish Region, a further fifteen were originally put on the 1954 Programme, later cancelled. For reasons now unclear the North Eastern Region initially indented for twenty on the 1956 Programme, and the Scottish Region could have found work for even more had steam continued. 72007 CLAN MACKINTOSH is at Carlisle Upperby (where no Clan was ever stationed) in 1963. The first five Clans, allocated to Glasgow Polmadie, had been withdrawn from service several months earlier, but not yet cut up. 72007 was allocated to Carlisle Kingmoor throughout its 13¾ year life.

Several of the smaller (that is, narrow firebox) BR Standard classes were directly derived from pre-1948 LMS antecedents, yet managed to portray a distinctive and attractive image in their own right. This was particularly true of the Standard Class 5 4-6-0, of which 73006 is seen on the turntable at Perth on 21 April 1952. Contrary to appearances the engine is not brand new, having entered traffic nearly one year earlier, in June 1951. Photograph J. Robertson, The Transport Treasury.

5 4-6-0s were also trimmed off the order for fifty, which goes some way to accounting for the curious final total of 172 engines in that class. Meanwhile the thirty-three engines still outstanding from the 1954 Programme (Class 4 4-6-0s Nos.75080-75089, Class 3 2-6-0s Nos.77020-77024, and 2-6-2Ts Nos.82045-82062) were finally cancelled in September 1956.

Later during that same month the last Standards were authorised with reluctance, thirty 2-10-0s, Nos.92221-92250, from Crewe on the 1958 Programme, in succession to Nos.92203-92220 from Swindon on the 1957 Programme agreed in December 1955. All forty-eight were for the Western Region to replace life-expired Churchward 28XX 2-8-0s (originally introduced in 1903) which at that time it was stated would be very expensive to maintain but for which there was no viable diesel alternative, as this would have entailed uneconomic double heading when compared to steam working. There was a certain irony in that the only steam locomotives to be sanctioned after the 1956 Programme were for the one region which had already set a date for the elimination of steam working, and the only one to have reacted against the Standards in general and the 9Fs in particular. (For good measure to its most senior officer, Keith Grand, to whom the Standards were anathema, would fall the honour of ceremonially unveiling the last one, No.92220 EVENING STAR, at Swindon Works in March 1960).

Six months earlier a paradox existed; although it was hoped to terminate steam locomotive construction by the end of 1958, it was not intended to order main line diesels in quantity until 1960. These could not be expected to begin to arrive for another year or so after that, but meanwhile the BR locomotive fleet had to be 'refreshed', to use the contemporary parlance. This meant that life-expired steam locomotives had to be routinely replaced by something. In April 1956 the Regional General Managers were requested 'to make an assessment of the minimum number of new locomotives considered essential to maintain and improve services, stating requirements in terms of steam and, alternatively, diesel locomotives each year (from 1958) up to and including the 1960 Programme'.

Interestingly, three regions, the London Midland, Scottish, and North Eastern, responded positively in terms of their estimated steam requirements, which were *(below)*:

There are some surprises here, not least forty Clans for the NE Region, additional to the twenty provisionally indented for on the 1956 Programme. The Region's philosophy was that the East Coast Main Line electrification, which in the mid-1950s was regarded as 'imminent' south of Doncaster, would eventually be progressed north of there and so provided little justification for short-term dieselisation. However, it is difficult to divine what role was envisaged for the somewhat effete Clan in an area long accustomed to much more powerful three-cylinder 2-6-2s and 4-6-2s, about fifty of the latter being of quite recent construction. There was no obvious ex-LNER type which it would seemingly supersede. One might have also have expected the NE to have required additional 9Fs to

Region	**1958**	**1959**	**1960**	**Total**
LMR	40 9F 2-10-0s	35 9F 2-10-0s	35 9F 2-10-0s	110
	15 5MT 4-6-0s	45 5MT 4-6-0s	46 5MT 4-6-0s	106
		19 2MT 2-6-0s	14 2MT 2-6-0s	33
ScR		17 6MT 4-6-2s	16 6MT 4-6-2s	33
		16 4MT 2-6-0s	8 4MT 2-6-0s	24
		14 3MT 2-6-0s	10 3MT 2-6-0s	24
NER		15 6MT 4-6-2s	25 6MT 4-6-2s	40
Total	**55**	**161**	**154**	**370**

Class 4 2-6-0s 76070 and 76000 (the latter's torrid journey north is recorded elsewhere in these pages, under 'The Airfix Moguls') at Motherwell on 2 June 1957. Aesthetically they were a very considerable improvement indeed upon their ugly Ivatt LMS predecessors. Photograph W. Hermiston, The Transport Treasury.

replace ageing ex-North Eastern 0-8-0s. Again, surprisingly, the Scottish Region also desired more Clans which, in conjunction with the putative Nos.72010-72019, would have brought its allocation up to fifty-three by say, 1962.

As usual the lion's share was for the LMR, with no fewer than 110 2-10-0s and 106 Class 5 4-6-0s, *both* of which could well have been of the Caprotti variety, as will be seen later. There was no mention of 4-6-2s but in *British Railways Standard Steam Locomotives* (p.111) E.S. Cox ten years on remarked that the question of building sister engines to No.71000 was actively debated in 1956.

Although largely hypothetical these figures, in conjunction with the 1956 'A' Programme, and the cancelled '1954' engines, do give some insight into how the British Railways Standard steam fleet might have further expanded by the early 1960s, to nearly 1,600 units, but for the change in traction policy announced in 1955. Would there also have been the possibility of any other Standard steam locomotive designs, or new variants of those already in existence?

***

As it was all the Standards had either six or ten coupled wheels, but none had eight. While there was never the remotest chance of a BR Standard Class 10 4-8-4, initially it was proposed to build a Class 8 2-8-2, which of course duly emerged as the celebrated 9F 2-10-0. The latter in turn prompted thoughts of a 4-8-0, but adverse reaction to it in one quarter before it had even appeared also nearly resulted in the construction of a Standard 2-8-0.

In his preface to Martin Evans' *Pacific Steam – the British Pacific Locomotive*, published in 1961, R.A. Riddles mused: '*a natural development for passenger work would have been a 4-8-0, with wide firebox, with powers of bank climbing, acceleration and deceleration, and possibly automatic stokers making an outlet for the surplus small coal now lying in stacks of millions of tons*'. The present writer thereupon wrote on this issue to Mr Riddles, who subsequently replied in May 1962, 'I had in mind a 4-8-0 for the Scottish Region for passenger work which could have been a good mixed traffic loco. Other than this at the time of my retirement no other types or classes were then contemplated.'

In fact only a few weeks after his slightly premature departure in September 1953 a proposed Standard Class 8F 2-8-0 was outlined, at the behest of his successor R.C. Bond. Although never mentioned by Cox, Roland Bond did refer to this in his own memoirs *A Lifetime with Locomotives* (1975) although somewhat coyly he did not identify the Region which prompted it. Of the initial batch of thirty 2-10-0s approved on the 1953 Programme, the first twenty no less were originally earmarked for the Western Region to replace the oldest units of the Churchward 28XX class 2-8-0s which were now approaching the fifty year mark and therefore life-expired. The WR was less than enthusiastic about its allocation of new Class 7 4-6-2s in 1951-52, and under its Chief, K.W.C. Grand, a dyed-in-the-wool ex-GWR man, started a rearguard action in opposition to the very prospect of having the new (and untried) 2-10-0 imposed upon it. The last 2-8-0s had been built in 1942 and eleven years later and five years into nationalisation the WR made a strong case to build new ones, pointing out it could do so for about 60 per cent of the equivalent cost of a BR 2-10-0, and for which total annual operating costs would be lower. (For good measure it also seems to have pressed to build additional 'Manor' 4-6-0s, despite the fact that Swindon was already building BR Class 4 4-6-0s; remarkably sanction *was* granted as late as 1953 for a further twenty Hawksworth 16XX 0-6-0PTs).

During November 1953 *two* outline schemes were prepared for Standard Class 8 2-8-0s. That at Derby was for a truncated version of the 9F with a similar, but shorter wide firebox boiler. The alternative, produced at the late Railway Executive headquarters in Marylebone, was for a narrow firebox engine derived directly from the

The smaller-boilered Class 3 2-6-0 was almost identical with the Class 4 Mogul below the running board and was generally considered to be the least appealing of the BR Standards. Not one has survived in preservation. Here the 'class leader', 77000 itself, strikes a particularly unflattering pose beneath a typical layer of 1950s BR locomotive grime, at Hull Borough Gardens shed on 4 August 1956. It had been 77001 which had posed, immaculate, for the official class portrait at Swindon 2½ years earlier.

Standard Class 5 4-6-0. Both showed a sharp drop in the level of the running board behind the outside cylinders, unlike all the previous BR Standards. By this time the first 2-10-0 was approaching completion at Crewe, and a total of 97 had already been authorised. However in early December 1953 the Works & Equipment Committee minuted (a proposed) 'alteration in standard range of steam locomotives, providing for the restriction of construction of Class 9 2-10-0 heavy freight locomotives to those at present under construction, together with such number already authorised as can immediately be justified by traffic requirements and operating economy. *Standard Class 8 locomotive to be designed for use on all Regions'.* [Author's emphasis.]

Yet only two months later it was proposed to order twenty further 2-10-0s from contractors for delivery in 1955. Although this was later rescinded there was still no obvious cutback on the existing orders for 9Fs! This was further augmented in February 1955 by the desire to order 101 more on the 1956 Programme, but strangely in addition there were to be five Class 8 2-8-0s (93000-93004) to be built at Swindon for the WR. In the event production design never commenced on either version, for it was no doubt considered unjustified to incur the expense of designing and tooling up for a new steam locomotive class by this time. An additional five

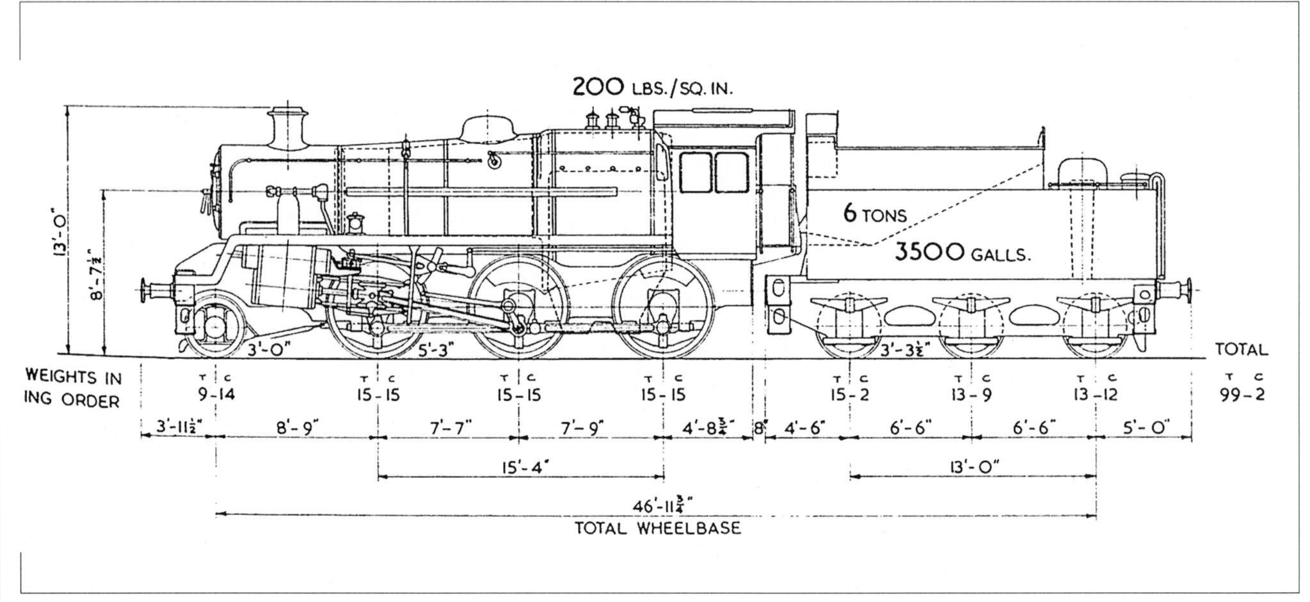

Original outline scheme for Class 3 2-6-0 as drafted at Swindon in 1949; note lower running board, conforming with that of the corresponding 2-6-2T, to give a much more pleasing result.

In contrast to the ugly Class 3 2-6-0 as built, the 2-6-2T version had a well balanced appearance, as typified by 82016 recorded at Eastleigh on 12 August 1955. Photograph W. Hermiston, The Transport Treasury.

2-10-0s were built instead, although not for the WR, and it is reasonable to assume that the forty-eight 9Fs reluctantly built for it under the 1957 and 1958 Programmes would otherwise have been BR 2-8-0s Nos.93005-93052.

About 1953, when the BR Crosti 2-10-0s were under design and there were high hopes for that project in terms of fuel economy, an outline sketch – no more – was got out showing a BR Standard Class 5 4-6-0 fitted with British Caprotti valve gear *and* a Crosti boiler! This was not progressed

Weight diagrams of the alternative (tentatively) proposed BR Standard Class 8 2–8–0s outlined at BR Headquarters (upper) and in Derby Development Office (lower) in November 1953. In the event neither option was taken any further.

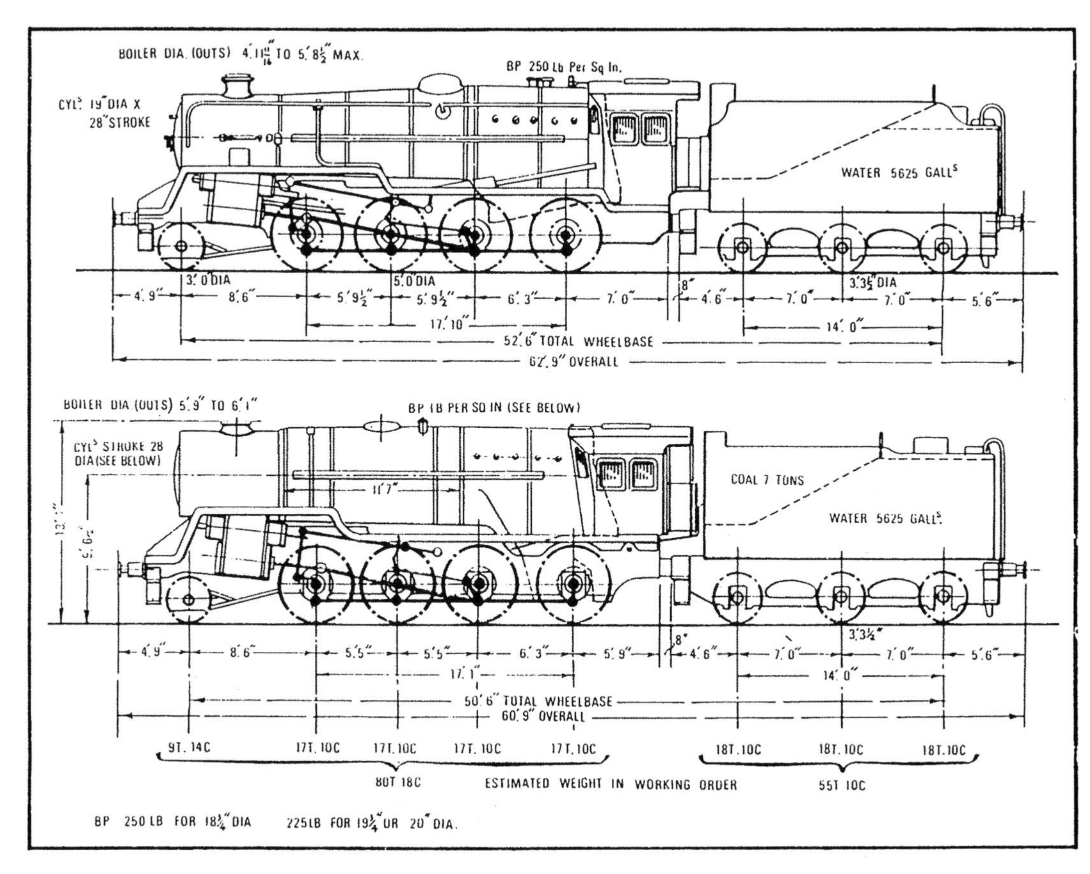

but thirty 4-6-0s equipped with this valve gear were later turned out of Derby Works during 1956-57. The *prime* objective was to reduce routine valve maintenance on shed, with the added bonus of a possible 5 per cent saving in coal consumption. E.S. Cox remarked that had steam continued British Caprotti valve gear would have received a wider application. Its manufacturers, Associated Locomotive Equipment Ltd of Worcester, submitted quotations for 30, 60 and 90 sets to BR in early 1955 for application to the 9F 2-10-0, of which over 100 had recently been sanctioned. A Caprotti 9F would have been an intriguing prospect. While it would doubtless have been a *very* free running engine indeed, it has to be said that the sharp exhaust, in conjunction with the shallow wide firebox might not have been in the best interests of fuel economy.

With the continuing decline in the quality of available coal some fine tuning to the smokebox arrangements on several classes, including some of the Standards, was undertaken. Double chimneys began to appear on the 2-10-0s and Class 4 4-6-0s in 1957, and in early 1958 Doncaster produced all the necessary drawings to modify the Standard Class 5 4-6-0 with double blastpipes and double chimneys. Four engines, Nos.73002, 73019, 73038 and 73046, were actually specifically earmarked to be fitted up for trial, one of each pair being allocated to the respective LM and WR

Actual British Railways Standard Steam Locomotive Building Programmes 1951-1955, notionally extended to 1960 on the basis of actual documentation.

Programme(s)	1951-53	1954	1955	1956(A)	1957	(1958-60)
Class 9F 2-10-0	92000-29	92030-96	-	92097-197	-	92198-*(307)*
(Class 8F 2-8-0)	-	-	-	*(93000-4?)*	*(93005-22?)*	*(93023-52?)*
Class 8 4-6-2	71000	-	-	-	-	-
Class 7MT 4-6-2	70000-54	-	-	*(70055-90)*	-	-
Class 6MT 4-6-2	72000-9	*72010-24*	-	*(72025-44)*	-	*(72045-117)*
Class 5MT 4-6-0	73000-44	73075-89	73090-124	73125-75	-	*(73176-281)*
Class 4MT 4-6-0	75000-79	*75080-9*	-	*(75090-119)*	-	-
Class 4MT 2-6-0	76000-44	76045-74	-	76075-119	-	*(76120-43)*
Class 3MT 2-6-0	77000-19	*77020-4*	-	*(77025-37)*	-	*(77038-61)*
Class 2MT 2-6-0	78000-44	78045-54	-	78055-64	-	*(78065-97)*
Class 4MT 2-6-4T	80000-115	80116-30	-	80131-*85*	-	-
Class 3MT 2-6-2T	82000-44	*82045-62*	-	*(82063-72)*	-	-
Class 2MT 2-6-2T	84000-29	-	-	*(84030-9)*	-	-

Total 1,576 locomotives.
If steam *had* continued more engines would assuredly have been built under the 1957 Programme bringing the total up to approximately 1,700.
If the Standard Class 8F 2-8-0 had not been built in lieu of 9F 2-10-0s the latter would have been numbered up to *92360*.

The BR Standard Class 4 2-6-4T cut a clean, modern outline. The emergence of 80154 from Brighton Works in March 1957 marked the completion of precisely 800 2-6-4Ts of LMS and BR design over a period of almost thirty years, and the first Fowler engines would be withdrawn only two years later. 80057 is at Polmadie, on 14 April 1956. Photograph J. Robertson, The Transport Treasury.

In a glorious picture, push and pull fitted Class 2 2-6-2T 84001 blows off at Chester on 6 September 1955. Photograph J. Robertson, The Transport Treasury.

75077

78040
78040

sheds in Bristol and Chester, but the project was stillborn. Similarly Doncaster had even prepared drawings in October 1957 for a double exhaust arrangement for the Class 4 2-6-4Ts, whose outward appearance would thereby have been greatly altered, but without positive result.

By this time, although new 2-10-0s continued to appear, interest in steam development on BR was waning fast. In 1959 there were half-hearted proposals, largely on the part of the Austrian inventor, to fit three Standard Class 5 4-6-0s with the Giesl oblong ejector, although his (unrealised) dream was to equip a Stratford-based Britannia Pacific. Although there had been pious pleas to get the best value out of the BR steam locomotive fleet in its declining years, in reality there was little evidence of this despite spare boilers being built for several classes up to 1961. By the following year, when withdrawal of the first Standards took place, it had been decided to eliminate steam traction on British Railways by 1972. This was very quickly brought forward to 1967, but (characteristically) once again things did not go quite according to plan and there were to be a few more months grace. Britannia No.70013 OLIVER CROMWELL was the last BR steam locomotive to receive a scheduled heavy repair, at Crewe Works in late 1966 (when theoretically it should have been repainted in the newly introduced BR blue). This made its ceremonial final run on 11 August 1968, barely twenty years after the BR Standard range had first been outlined in E.S. Cox's historic initial report of June 1948.

Top left. **The Class 4 4-6-0 was closely related – in its boiler and cylinders – to the 2-6-4T but in spirit was actually a throwback to an abortive LMS Stanier 1934 proposal for a 'light' 4-6-0 for Scotland. Nine months old, 75077 with large BR1B tender is at Folkestone on 14 August 1956; though all eighty were built at Swindon, the last actually to appear was 75064 in June 1957. It was also the last 4-6-0 to be built anywhere in the world; in fact most other countries had long since abandoned the type for new construction. Photograph J. Robertson, The Transport Treasury.**

Bottom left. **Class 2 Mogul 78040 basking in the sun at Wigan (the old L&Y shed, near-ruined by colliery subsidence) on 2 June 1957. The Class 2 2-6-0s and 2-6-2Ts were the smallest of the BR Standard classes and were, obviously, closely derived from the respective Ivatt LMS designs introduced in 1946. Photograph The Transport Treasury.**

Below. **The magnificent 9F 2-10-0 is represented by 92170; new to traffic on the last day of 1957 it is on Doncaster shed nearly six months later, actually showing some evidence of cleaning! It was this variant, with single chimney and high capacity BR1F tender which, arguably, performed the most distinctive duties of the class, the sharply timed Annesley-Woodford 'runners', during 1957-1965. Photograph J. Robertson, The Transport Treasury.**

'Something Different'

Above and below. The rest of the Standards, despite their bold new looks, were in many ways straightforward replacements of existing designs – the 2-10-0 was something different'. So wrote P. Atkins in *The British Railways Standard 9F 2-10-0* (Irwell Press 1993). And they were different enough for BR to put on a real show, outside Crewe Paint Shop on 21 May 1954. 92000-92003 were on display for inspection by the technical press. Ancient 'Cauliflower' 0-6-0 was thoughtfully placed alongside 92000 if any emphasis was needed concerning the march of progress.

92000
To traffic 5/1/54
Tender: Type BR1G No.949 BR1G No.1513.
SHEDS
Ebbw Junction 1/54
Bath Green Park 6/61
Banbury 9/61
Old Oak Common 3/62
Tyseley 7/62
Bristol Barrow Road 12/62
Gloucester Horton Road 2/65

REPAIRS
20/10/54-5/11/54**U** Swindon
3/5/56-10/5/56**U** Swindon
1/8/56-8/8/56**U** Swindon
6/10/56-18/12/56**LC** Swindon
11/8/59-3/60**HG** Swindon
Condemned 7/65; stored at Gloucester Horton Road
Cut up Birds, Long Marston 11/65

92060
To traffic 5/11/55
Weather shields, Steam operated cylinder cocks, Westinghouse Air Compressor fitted.
Tender: Type BR1B No.1149
30/12/60 BR1B No.1307

SHEDS
Tyne Dock 5/11/55
Wellingborough 16/12/55
Tyne Dock 27/3/56

REPAIRS
17/1/57-28/1/57**NC** Gateshead
23/3/59-29/4/59**G** Darlington
11/8/60-7/10/60**CL** Darlington
10/3/61-20/6/61**H** Darlington
15/7/63-29/9/63**G** Crewe
27/11/64-2/1/65**CL** Crewe
Condemned 23/10/66; stored Tyne Dock shed 10/66-3/67
Cut up at Drapers, Hull 4/67

Right and below. **There were of course, well documented and fascinating variations among the 9Fs. Best-known were the Crostis, loathed at Wellingborough and disappointing in the extent to which the pre-heater improved efficiency or rather, didn't. To the despair of the eponymous Signor, the savings were never enough to trigger the hoped-for royalty payments – the Franco-Crosti boiler (to give it its correct name) while proving efficacious on older, inherently inefficient designs, could do little for a boiler like the standard No.9, a boiler which was as efficient, more or less, as it was possible to be. Modifications did not help and after variously lengthy periods in store at Wellingborough they were rebuilt for conventional working between 1959 and 1962. 92022 was out of use for nearly three years! Both the Crostis shown here are in the 'second phase' with redesigned exhaust and smoke deflector; 92027 is in the shed yard at Oxford on 20 May 1956 and 92024 inside one of the Wellingborough roundhouses earlier in the year, on 2 April. They were heartily detested. Photographs R.S. Carpenter Collection.**

A couple of 'one-offs'. 92220 EVENING STAR, the last BR steam locomotive, was named in a special ceremony at Swindon on 18 March 1960. A few weeks later, on 2 April 1960, it was at Old Oak Common having worked an LCGB special the day before; now it was booked to work a freight to Cardiff, where it would take up residence at Canton. The other 'one-off' was 92250, with its Giesl ejector. Given the vagaries of everyday running and fuel quality the couple of percentage points in economy was effectively negligible and though the ejector (put on in 1959) was scheduled to come off in the summer of 1960, in the event it stayed in place until the end. In Michael Mensing's picture 92250 is on an up part-fitted freight at Lapworth troughs on the Birmingham-Leamington main line, 20 September 1961. Photographs R.C. Riley, The Transport Treasury and Michael Mensing.

92100
To traffic 30/7/56
Additional handwritten information of the front of the card:-
Steam operated cylinder cocks/fitted with internal gauge frame pipes.
G & C gradual brake valve for engine & train.
G & C ejector valve for train.
Tender: Type BR1C No.1310 BR1F No.1386

SHEDS
Toton 30/7/56
Leicester (Midland) 22/3/58
Toton 12/12/59
Westhouses 30/1/60
Wellingborough 9/3/63
Leicester (Midland) 18/5/63
Birkenhead 25/4/64

REPAIRS
4/8/60-24/8/60**CL** Gorton
16/8/61-21/9/61**HC** Crewe
13/8/63-16/10/63**HG** Crewe
9/9/64-24/10/64**LC** Crewe
In pencil on back of card: Collision Dam.Spl 4/5/67, 54000, Can.Dec. 11/5/67, into shops? cutting up.

MILEAGE

1956	11,739
1957	28,295
1958	31,431
1959	23,970
1960	19,926

Withdrawn 5/67, stored at Birkenhead shed 5-8/67 and Crewe (South) shed 9-11/67, scrapped at Cohens, Kettering, winter 1967-1968

Ten 9Fs, 92060-92066 and 92097-92099, had air pumps for the Consett iron ore trains from Tyne Dock. The first batch all went to Wellingborough on loan, instead of Tyne Dock (though the air pump brackets were fitted) for a while, from December 1955 to February-March 1956, covering for the Crostis then being modified. They then went on to Crewe for the pumps to be fitted, before going to Tyne Dock where they stayed. The second three got the pumps from new and went direct to Tyne Dock where they also stayed for their working lives. A date is given for this fine portrait of 92098, 3 August 1958, though there is no indication as to the shed where she is turning. It's *not* Tyne Dock but, where? From the A4 tender in the background and the distinctive roof it is possible to make a comparison with photographs published in BRILL (*The Carlisle Canal A3s* for instance, January 1999); the unexpected location, it turns out, is Haymarket, Edinburgh. Photograph W. Hermiston, The Transport Treasury.

92200
To traffic 18/11/58
Tender: Type BR1F No.1410

SHEDS
Doncaster 18/11/58
Immingham 9/63
Doncaster 6/64
Langwith Junction 6/65

REPAIRS
No details
Condemned 10/65, stored at Langwith (Junction) shed 10-11/65, scrapped at Wards, Killamarsh 12/65

Right. A beautiful 9F, 92010 at March shed, 22 May 1955, where it had been since new the previous year. The fine buffer beam shows up against the overall coating of grime; confirmation maybe, of a popular suspicion, that some sheds painted them up to convince crews that an engine had been for overhaul... Photograph J. Robertson, The Transport Treasury.

Below. 92140, a 9F in the condition we all came to know and love – indescribably filthy with even the half-heartedly wiped cab number fading fast under yet more layers. This is New England shed, 3 February 1962. ER crews took to the Standards straight away, appreciating the power and the riding, particularly on the 9F, though there were some reservations about the draughty cab. The best use of 9Fs was on the Annesley-Woodford 'windcutters', 68 miles each way in less than eight hours by Annesley men, out and home. The 9Fs were used to great advantage, too, on the Doncaster-New England and New England-Ferme Park coal trains, but not with such punctuality and efficiency as on the GC. Photograph A.G. Ellis, The Transport Treasury.

Below right. 92205 clumps north after passing through the station at Huddersfield in the 1960s. The outline of Huddersfield ('Hillhouse') shed coaling plant can just be discerned ahead – just at the right of the distant signal gantry. 92205 was one of the few 9Fs that had been based of a time on the Southern, at Eastleigh and Feltham from 1960 to 1963. Before that it had been a Western Region engine. This view is probably about 1966-67, when it was based at Wakefield. The top middle lamp bracket on the tender, it can be noted, is the original WR pattern. Photograph The Transport Treasury.

92010

72000 CLAN BUCHANAN in fine condition at its home shed Polmadie (that's the high Repair Shop in the background) on 26 April 1952. The engine, only three months or so old and the whole class only just into traffic, looks fit as a fiddle, coal piled high and ready to go, purring with just the odd whiff of steam. The record is lost, alas, of who 72000's Driver and Fireman might be; John Robertson haunted sheds like Haymarket and Polmadie and was very well known to crews and shed staff alike. He frequently took portraits like this and handed copies round. Does a wrinkled copy of this one still exist in someone's treasured family collection? Photograph J. Robertson, The Transport Treasury.

Glorious view at Carlisle Citadel, 4 September 1953. 72000 CLAN BUCHANAN is on a down Glasgow to Liverpool and Manchester train (the sort of workings with which they became closely associated) while 46103 ROYAL SCOTS FUSILIER waits with a St Enoch-Leeds express. Photograph M.N. Bland, The Transport Treasury.

THE CLASSY CLANS

Self-confessed Clan admirer RUSSELL NEWLAND, a leading light of the campaign to build HENGIST anew, indulges in a personal rumination on the Clan story.

Just over 50 years ago the last BR Standard Clan 4-6-2 left Crewe Works to start its all-to brief service career on the still new British Railways. BR 72009 CLAN STEWART was never meant to be the last of the class but circumstances were to prove particularly unkind to this most misunderstood of Standard types. The Class 6 Pacific came about from an operating requirement for a more powerful locomotive than the 5MT types then in use, a 6MT with higher route availability than a class 7, and able to cope with inferior quality fuel, hence the wide firebox. After a design for a Class 5 Pacific was rejected, a compromise Class 6 was produced and accepted, influenced no doubt by the success of West Country 34004 YEOVIL during the 1948 Locomotive Interchange. The choice of names came from E.S. Cox's desire to commemorate the then near-extinct ex-HR 4-6-0 'Clans'. Authorised in November 1949 all were built at Crewe (Lot 221) and were released to traffic between the end of December 1951 and March 1952. 72000-72004 were allocated to Polmadie (66A) and 72005-72009 to Carlisle Kingmoor (68A). For maintenance Crewe Works initially had responsibility but this was transferred to St. Rollox in 1956 and finally to Cowlairs in the spring of 1958.

Whether they were ever officially tagged 'Baby Brits' is not known but in essence the design was a scaled down Britannia with a smaller boiler, lower boiler pressure (225lb) and smaller cylinders, most other parts being interchangeable. A taller chimney kept the overall height the same but from a distance the average spotter had trouble telling the difference between the two classes. BR1 'inset' tenders were attached as per the first batches of Britannias.

The 6MT Clans had a chequered career with BR, seemingly liked or loathed at turns. It depended on who you spoke to and at what stage in the engines' working life the chat took place. However, their good points far outweighed the bad and they were well-liked by their regular crews. They were mainly placed on Glasgow to Crewe, Manchester and Liverpool trains on the West Coast and Edinburgh-Leeds and Carlisle-Bradford trains via the Settle & Carlisle, but became associated in particular with Stranraer, which they reached either by way of Dumfries or, in roundabout fashion, Ayr and Girvan. It was there in the south-western corner of Scotland, in parts as remote and wild as anywhere in these islands, and in some of the worst weather conditions to be found within them, that for more than a decade the Clans put in work of the highest order. It was along the fierce switchback south of Girvan, in particular, that the Clans came to be highly regarded. It is a thread that runs through the history of the class, their competence and surefootedness on adverse gradients.

A lot was made of the fact that they never took up the duties on the Highland routes they were originally intended for, but along with most of the Standard classes they were completed behind schedule and by the time they were ready a brand new batch of Stanier Black 5s had been allocated to the area, so the Clans were diverted to Glasgow and Carlisle. Late completion also meant that they missed their slot at the Rugby Testing

72001 CLAN CAMERON in the shed yard at Newton Heath on 15 March 1953. While the Clans were daily visitors to Lancashire over many years, photographs of them at this end of their operating 'axis' are far from common. The time of day might have had something to do with it – presumably the 'layover' at Newton Heath or Bank Hall came during the middle of the day; during the working week there would have been few visitors at such times. Come the weekend when the spotters arrived, the Clans would be safely tucked up in Carlisle and Glasgow! Photograph M.N. Bland, The Transport Treasury.

Contrast in front ends; there is no date or location attached to this photograph, though Kingmoor or Upperby would be a reasonable bet... By way of an aside, CLAN MACGREGOR was the first Clan to visit Bristol, turning up out of the blue on 9 July 1960. It returned north the following day. It had had something of a trek, enough to warrant comment in the railway press; on the afternoon of 7 July it had been at Stirling and once it had started out, covered the 468 miles in 31 hours, at an average speed of 15mph. Photograph The Transport Treasury.

Station, something that was to cause the class a few problems.

As more crews got used to them they started to turn up very far from home at Aberdeen, Inverness, Port Talbot, Newcastle and Bristol, visiting London more often than is still generally realised. 72001 CLAN CAMERON remains the only Pacific type to have worked over the West Highland Line (May/June 1956) and 72009 CLAN STEWART was tried out for a month in late 1958 on the Eastern Region at Stratford working from Liverpool Street to Clacton and Norwich (part of a failed plot to transfer five Clans to the ER in exchange for their beloved Britannias). They were also extensively used on freight and parcels workings during their careers as well as numerous specials; some moved depots, with Haymarket and St. Margarets playing host between 1958 and 1960. More varied work was allocated to them as their versatility was better appreciated. These included portions of the 'Thames Clyde Express', the 'St. Mungo', the 'Night Scotsman' and 'Queen of Scots Pullmans' and deputising for the many failed diesels that plagued the network at the time.

Class 7 and 8 locomotives came north in 1961 after dieselisation had displaced them further south, causing the Clans to be downgraded to secondary work. The Scottish Region had its big 'purge' of 'non-standard' steam types in late 1962, when among 213 locomotives withdrawn were Nos.72000-72004. After moving first to Glasgow Parkhead they were stored and stripped of all useful 'spares'. They were eventually moved to Darlington for scrapping in early 1964. The Kingmoor quintet survived intact until 1965, working over their deceased classmates' routes, visiting Polmadie regularly. As they came up for overhaul they were in turn withdrawn. Some of their final workings involved troop trains on the 'Port Road' between Carlisle and Stranraer, the last trains to run on that line before it was closed. When 72006 CLAN MACKENZIE, withdrawn in the May, fell to the cutters' torch in August 1966 it rendered the class extinct. This locomotive served BR for only 14 years 3 months, the longest serving Clan, and also gained the highest yearly mileage for the class, 70,699 miles in 1956.

Overall the Clans left some differing memories with BR crews, shed staff and observers alike. Limited in numbers – only ten – and confined mostly to the north west and Scotland and only occasionally working top-link services, they spent most of their short careers out of the limelight and were quite 'camera shy'. Some crews rated them the most surefooted of any Pacifics that they had worked with, preferring the Clan to a Britannia or a rebuilt Royal Scot. Others, especially at 'foreign' MPDs, found them difficult to handle and this got them a bad reputation. Something that has to be realised is the way the class was seen by the shed staff and crews who worked them; even railway observers of the day saw a 'Pacific' and expected greyhound performances. At first they were mistakenly allocated Class 7 duties and could not keep to the faster, tighter timings. As a result there were complaints ranging from bad steaming to a lack of pulling power; indifferent handling and incorrect firing techniques made the situation worse. Word got about and the class were labelled as a problem, and not something a crew wanted to see rostered against their name on a dark winters morning! E.S. Cox discerned a distinct 'wooliness' in their steaming and some modifications were carried out in 1954, most notably to the diameter of the blastpipe, resulting in improved steaming and increased power. Indeed enough information was gathered to allow a 'Mark 2' version to be planned with modifications to make a better locomotive. This became

72000 CLAN BUCHANAN

Date to traffic 29/12/51
Steam operated cylinder cocks
G and C gradual brake valve for engine and train
G and C ejector valve for train
Tender: Type BR1 No.784

SHEDS
Polmadie 29/12/51
Haymarket 25/10/57
Polmadie 16/4/58
St. Margarets 23/11/59
Polmadie 21/3/60

REPAIRS
1/1/52-8/1/**52NC(EO)** Crewe Weighing and painting
3/10/52-4/10/52**NC(EO)** St Rollox 44,272 44,164
24/11/52-20/12/52**LC** Crewe 51,937 51,829
16/3/53-21/3/53**LC** St Rollox 64,057 10,369
BW1533 fitting of draught excluders
13/8/53-28/8/53**LC(EO)** St Rollox 91,288
14/1/54-10/2/54**LI** Crewe 111,644 1,721
4/10/54-8/10/54**LC(EO)** St Rollox 40,391
19/12/55-1/3/56**HG** Crewe 87,382 380
E2943 Alterations to frames & spring bracket
R3208 Elimination of steam drier
R3345 Atomiser modified
R4194 New type drain plugs on Timken R' Bearing axleboxes
R4906 New chimney exhaust ring, petticoat & bl'stpipe cap
2/10/57-3/10/57**LC** St Rollox
14/11/57-5/12/57**LC(EO)** St Rollox
14/8/58-13/9/58**HI** St Rollox 119,900
17/3/60-19/3/60**HC(EO)** Cowlairs
5/11/60-11/2/61**HG** Cowlairs 88,966
29/10/62 stored

BOILERS
826 from new
832 1/3/56
964 11/2/61

ANNUAL MILEAGE
1951 108
1952 53,580
1953 56,205
1954 51,401
1955 37,322
1956 45,565
1957 44,730
1958 40,912
1959 43,014
1960 35,025
1961 33,212
1962 25,614
Condemned 29/12/62.
Stored at Polmadie 10/62-5/63, Parkhead 5-9/63, Darlington Scrap Yard 10/63-3/64. Cut up 3/64.

72001 CLAN CAMERON

To traffic 29/12/51
G and C gradual brake valve for engine and train
G and C ejector valve for train
Tender: Type BR1 No.785

SHEDS
Polmadie 29/12/51
Haymarket loan 11/59
Polmadie 21/3/60

REPAIRS
9/9/52-12/9/52**NC** St Rollox 36,862 36,723
5/12/52-20/1/53**LC(EO)** Crewe 58,538 8,399
BW1533 fitting of draught exluders
17/7/53-18/9/53**LI**
88,518
R5442 Alteration to pony truck lubricators
5764/8 provision of padded back to fireman's seat
5764/9 attention to pony truck lubrication
5764/2 providing stops to prevent jamming of reversing gear
R5400 manganese liners to intermediate rubbing plates and buffer
12/10/54-16/10/54**LC(EO)** St Rollox 69,241
4/5/55-14/6/55**HI** Crewe 95,127 15,844
R4194 New type drain plugs and Timken Roller Bearing axleboxes
21/1/57-30/1/57**LC(EO)** St Rollox
13/3/57-18/4/57**HG** St Rollox 93,393
2/4/58-12/4/58**LC** St Rollox
4/12/58-20/12/58**LI** Cowlairs 77,173
17/2/60-19/3/60**HC(EO)** Cowlairs
21/4/61-17/6/61**HI** Cowlairs 93,926
11/10/62-13/10/62**LC** Cowlairs

BOILERS
827 from new
835 18/4/57
830 19/3/60

ANNUAL MILEAGE
1951 139
1952 58,339
1953 50,037
1954 59,226
1955 50,220
1956 50,868
1957 47,689
1958 38,098
1959 44,013
1960 39,414
1961 34,034
1962 23,495
Condemned 29/12/62.
Stored Polmadie 10/62-5/63, Parkhead 5-9/63, Darlington Scrap Yard 10/63-2/64.
Cut up 2/64.

72002 CLAN CAMPBELL

To traffic 14/1/52
G and C gradual brake valve for engine and train
G and C ejector valve for train
Tender: Type BR1 No.786

SHEDS
Polmadie 14/1/52
Haymarket 25/10/57
Polmadie 19/4/58
Haymarket Loan 11/59
Polmadie 21/3/60

REPAIRS
1/9/52-6/9/52**NC(EO)** St Rollox 43,574 43,574
8/1/53-17/1/53**LC(EO)**St Rollox 66,419 1,473
9/3/53-14/3/53**LC** St Rollox 73,813 8,867
BW1533 fitting of draught excluders
21/1/54-25/2/54**LI** Crewe 121,781 3,307
19/5/55**NC** St Rollox
29/7/55-20/8/55**LC(EO)** St Rollox 74,646
23/1/56-29/3/56**HG** Crewe 92,275 2,075
R3345 atomiser modification
E2948 alteration frame and spring bracket
R4906 provision and fitting new chimney ejector exhaust ring, petticoat and blast pipe cap
BW 2087 modification blast pipe cap
R3208 Elimination of steam driers
1/10/57**LC** St Rollox
16/6/58-5/7/58**HI** Cowlairs 125,898
21/10/58-24/10/58**LC** Cowlairs
26/1/59-17/2/59**LC(EO)** Cowlairs
8/7/59-4/9/59**LC(EO)** Cowlairs
7/3/60-19/3/60**NC** Cowlairs
22/3/61-6/5/61**HG** Cowlairs 82,320
1/8/61-8/8/61**LC(EO)** Cowlairs

BOILERS
828 from new
833
826 29/3/56
832

ANNUAL MILEAGE
1952 64,946
1953 53,528
1954 53,229
1955 40,175
1956 52,182
1957 54,489
1958 41,926
1959 26,761
1960 30,087
1961 30,212
1962 32,716
Condemned 29/12/62.
Stored Polmadie 10/62-5/63, Parkhead 5-9/63, Darlington Scrap Yard 10/63-4/64.
Cut up 4/64.

72005 CLAN MACGREGOR at Kingmoor on 14 May 1961; Ivatt 2-6-0 43045 alongside has AWS already but not yet the Clan. Kingmoor's transfer to the LM in February 1958, supplanting Upperby as 12A, effectively prolonged the life of the class, for when the Scottish Region had its notorious 'cull' of 'non-standard' types (including those types that were merely small in number) in 1962, the half of the class on the LM could soldier on. Of course the ScR in any event might well have considered ten Clans unworthy of further work if Kingmoor had been retained but, however you look at it, it was a waste. Photograph The Transport Treasury.

known by its Crewe Works Order number, the now-famous Lot 242.

Nonetheless something of the air of failure stayed with the Clans throughout their working lives despite overall performances that were only just short of their designer's aims. The aim of all the BR Standards was to be hard working, of easy maintenance, have low running costs, high availability, and be able to carry out whatever duties were assigned. In all these respects all classes, especially the Clans, succeeded. The real reason behind their variable form is almost certainly the same as 71000 DUKE OF GLOUCESTER. They were constructed incorrectly, and that loco since being rebuilt has proved all the doubters wrong. Maybe the same will happen with HENGIST...

NO	NAME	REGION
72000	CLAN BUCHANAN	ScR
72001	CLAN CAMERON	ScR
72002	CLAN CAMPBELL	ScR
72003	CLAN FRASER	ScR
72004	CLAN MACDONALD	ScR
72005	CLAN MACGREGOR	ScR
72006	CLAN MACKENZIE	ScR
72007	CLAN MACKINTOSH	ScR
72008	CLAN MACLEOD	ScR
72009	CLAN STEWART	ScR
LOT 242		
72010	HENGIST	SR
72011	HORSA	SR
72012	CANUTE	SR
72013	WILDFIRE	SR
72014	FIREBRAND	SR
72015	CLAN COLQUHOUN	ScR
72016	CLAN GRAHAM	ScR
72017	CLAN MACDOUGALL	ScR
72018	CLAN MACLEAN	ScR
72019	CLAN DOUGLAS	ScR
72020	CLAN GORDON	ScR
72021	CLAN HAMILTON	ScR
72022	CLAN KENNEDY	ScR
72023	CLAN LINDSAY	ScR
72024	CLAN SCOTT	ScR

72006 CLAN MACKENZIE, AWS equipped, at Carlisle on 5 September 1961. Photograph R.F. Smith, The Transport Treasury.

72003 CLAN FRASER

To traffic 19/1/52
Steam operated cylinder cocks
G and C gradual brake valve for engine and train
G and C ejector valve for train
Fitted with BR plugs
Tender: Type BR1 No.787

SHEDS
Polmadie 19/1/52
St Margarets 5/11/59
Polmadie 21/3/60

REPAIRS
3/7/52-4/7/52**NC(EO)** St Rollox 22,383 22,383
15/11/52-1/12/**52LC(EO)** St Rollox 46,215 46,245
1/12/53-2/1/54**LI** Crewe 102,013 49,961
R3622 alteration to spring balancing arrangement and fitting of stops to prevent reversing gear jamming
10/9/54-17/9/54**LC(EO)** St Rollox 41,358
R3400, R3698 Modification to tank holding down arrangement
6/3/55-7/4/55**LC(EO)** shed 62,555
5/10/55-14/11/55**HI** Crewe 85,201 32,132
R4194 R3345 Atomiser modified
4/7/56**NC** St Rollox
7/12/56-18/12/56**LC(EO)** St Rollox
30/4/57-8/6/57**HG** St Rollox 74,263
E2948 alterations frame & spring bracket R49064
5731A Alteration to method of securing pins (grease lubricator)
5756 Provision of hinged cab front windows
5900 Saftey links between engine & tender
18/6/57-20/6/57**LC(EO)** St Rollox
27/10/58-15/11/58**LI** St Rollox 73,492
C50608 Safety chains in SC smokebox
9/7/59-17/7/59**LC(EO)** Cowlairs
18/1/60-23/1/60**NC** Cowlairs
5/12/60-30/12/60**HI** Cowlairs 90,865

BOILERS
829 from new
827 8/6/57

ANNUAL MILEAGE
1952 52,052
1953 49,961
1954 53,069
1955 38,212
1956 53,359
1957 44,983
1958 49,727
1959 49,393
1960 35,078
1961 31,881
1962 32,318
Condemned 29/12/62.
Stored Polmadie 10/62-5/63, Parkhead 5-9/63, Darlington Scrap Yard 10/63-3/64.
Cut up 3/64.

72004 CLAN MACDONALD

To traffic 2/2/52
Tender weather boards; steam operated cylinder cocks
Smokebox regulator; G and C gradual brake valve for engine and train
G and C ejector valve for train
Fitted with standard fusible and washout plugs
Tender: Type BR1 No.788

SHEDS
Polmadie 2/2/52
Haymarket 6/11/59
Polmadie 21/3/60

REPAIRS
20/3/52-2/5/52**LC(EO)** Crewe 3,691 3,691
12/12/52-31/12/52**LC(EO)** St Rollox 46,207
10/4/53-25/4/53**LC(EO)** St Rollox 61,315 15,099
27/4/53-2/5/53**LC(EO)** St Rollox 62,765 16,549
29/6/53-4/7/53**LC** St Rollox 67,876
BW1533 fitting of draught excluders
4/5/54-11/6/54**LI** Crewe 107,736 16,254
R3622 alteration to spring balancing arrangement and fitting of stops to prevent reversing gear jamming
R3242 alterations to pony truck lubricators
R3400 manganese liners to intermediate rubbing plates and intermediate buffer faces
3/9/54-8/9/54**LC(EO)** St Rollox 14,048
7/2/56-6/4/56**HI** Crewe 71,859 3,119
R3345 atomiser modification
R4906 provision and fitting new chimney ejector exhaust ring petticoat and blast pipe cap
17/9/57-19/10/57**HG** St Rollox 72,348
2/2/59-4/3/59 **HC(EO)** Cowlairs
25/1/60-28/1/60 **NC** Cowlairs
14/3/60, LC, **(EO)** Cowlairs
20/4/60-6/5/60**LC(EO)** Cowlairs
18/4/61-21/4/61**LC**
10/11/61-16/12/61**HG** Cowlairs 144,284

BOILERS
830 from new
829 10/57
828 16/12/61

ANNUAL MILEAGE
1952 46,216
1953 45,266
1954 46,464
1955 38,530
1956 43,054
1957 39,045
1958 49,559
1959 32,663
1960 33,930
1961 22,394
1962 35,385
Condemned 29/12/62.
Stored Polmadie 10/62-5/63, Parkhead 5-9/63, Darlington Scrap Yard 10/63-3/64.
Cut up 3/64.

72006 CLAN MACKENZIE, beautifully lit and way off its normal haunts. This is Old Oak Common(!) on 9 December 1963 and this particular classy Clan worked a special from Paddington later in the day. It had come south through Banbury with a London-bound freight on 29 November and went back north on the Midland, taking a Cricklewood-Carlisle freight on 15 December. Photograph Peter Groom.

72005 CLAN MACGREGOR

To traffic 19/2/52
Tender: Type BR1 No.789

SHEDS
Kingmoor 19/2/52
Haymarket 26/10/57
Kingmoor 19/4/58

REPAIRS

26/8/52-30/8/52**NC(EO)** St Rollox	36,841	36,841
11/2/53-21/2/53**LC(EO)** St Rollox	70,213	5,257
BW1533 draught excluders fitted		
10/9/54-14/10/54**HI** Crewe	162,187	35,866
R4194 fitting new type drain plugs on Timken roller bearing axleboxes		
R3622 alteration to spring balancing arrangement and fitting of stops to prevent reversing gear jamming		
R3242 alteration to pony truck lubricators		
R3400 manganese liners to intermediate rubbing plates and intermediate buffer faces		
30/4/56-20/7/56**HG** Crewe	93,384	17,961
R4906 provision and fitting chimney petticoat etc		
R5900 provision of safety links between engine & tender		
E2948 attention to frames and spring bracket		
R3208 Elimination of steam drier		
R3345 Atomiser modified		
4/8/56-7/9/56**LC(EO)** Crewe	1,759	19,720
12/11/57-30/11/57**LC(EO)** St Rollox	82,823	59,152
26/8/58-25/9/58**HI** Cowlairs	127,170	43,361
20/10/59-5/11/59**LC** Cowlairs		
10/3/60-12/3/60**NC(EO)** Cowlairs		
19/12/60-5/1/61**LC(EO)** Cowlairs	110,908	43,627
9/3/61-13/7/61**HG** Cowlairs	117,605	6,697

BOILERS
831 from new
838 20/7/56
833 13/7/61

ANNUAL MILEAGE
1952 64,956
1953 61,365
1954 46,884
1955 64,405
1956 41,632
1957 60,138
1958 58,940
1959 51,702
1960 43,627
Condemned 1/5/65.
Cut up West of Scotland Shipbreaking Co, Troon 7/65.

72006 CLAN MACKENZIE

To traffic 27/2/52
Steam operated cylinder cocks
G and C gradual brake valve for engine and train
G and C ejector valve for train
Tender: Type BR1 No.790

SHEDS
Kingmoor 27/2/52
Haymarket 26/10/57
Kingmoor 19/4/58

REPAIRS

15/12/52-16/1/53**LC** Crewe	61,178	61,178
22/4/54-29/5/54**LI**	145,623	19,408
R3622 alteration to spring balancing arrangement and fitting of stops to prevent reversing gear jamming		
R3242 alterations to pony truck lubricators		
R3400 manganese liners to intermediate rubbing plates and intermediate buffer faces		
R3682 fitting new type drawhook rubbers		
12/1/55-4/2/55**LC(EO)** Crewe	43,400	1,400
R4194 new type drain plugs on Timken roller bearing axleboxes		
14/11/55-18/1/56**HG** Crewe	93,453	51,453
R3345 atomiser modification		
E2948 attention to frames and spring bracket		
R4906 provision and fitting new chimney ejector, etc		
BW2087 modification to blast pipe cap		
9/5/57-10/5/57**NC(EO)** St Rollox	93,624	22,925
7/10/57-8/10/57**LC** St Rollox	122,039	51,340
26/2/58-5/4/58**HI** Cowlairs	136,486	4,662
15/1/59-7/2/59**HC(EO)** Cowlairs	41,188	806
4/6/59-3/7/59**LC(EO)** Cowlairs		
1/10/59-17/10/59**NC** Cowlairs		
20/1/60-24/3/60**LC(EO)** Cowlairs		
11/4/60-6/5/60**HC** Cowlairs		
20/5/61**HG** Cowlairs	128,046	6,837
21/6/61**LC(EO)** Cowlairs	1,221	8,058
29/6/61**LC**	9,423	2,586
13/7/61**LC**		
2/3/63**LC**		
28/9/63**HI** Cowlairs		
1/7/64-6/8/64**LC** Cowlairs		
8/2/65-2/4/65**LC(EO)** Cowlairs		

BOILERS
832 from new
833 18/1/56
832 20/5/61

ANNUAL MILEAGE
1952 61,178
1953 65,037
1954 61,408
1955 51,453
1956 70,699
1957 61,125
1958 45,044
1959 40,433
1960 40,394
Condemned 21/5/66.
Stored at Kingmoor 5-8/66, cut up J. McWilliams, Shettleston 10/66

Below. **72007 CLAN MACKINTOSH at Upperby, July 1963. Grime covers all, with not a trace of lining to be seen. Photograph The Transport Treasury.**

72007 CLAN MACKINTOSH

To traffic 4/3/52
Tender: BR1 No.791

SHEDS
Kingmoor 4/3/52

REPAIRS

23/3/53-28/3/53**LC** St Rollox	72,785	12,659
BW1533 fitting draught excluders "18/4/53"		
1/3/54-8/4/54**HI** Crewe	133,019	8,597
R3622 alteration to spring balancing arrangement and fitting of stops to prevent reversing gear jamming		
R3242 alterations to pony truck lubricators		
R3400 manganese liners to intermediate rubbing plates and intermediate buffer faces		
18/8/55-21/10/55**HG** Crewe	94,448	40,514
R4194 new type drain plugs on timken roller bearings		
R3345 atomiser modified		
E2948 attention to frames and spring bracket		
R3208 Elimination of steam drier		
5/2/57-21/2/57**LC(EO)** St Rollox	85,447	7,462
8/10/57-9/10/57**LC** St Rollox	122,462	44,477
28/11/57-10/1/58**HI** St Rollox	130,864	52,879
R5731/A alteration to method of securing pins (grease lubrication)		
R5742 new chimney		
R5777 "removal of down sanding"		
21/3/58-26/4/58**LC** Cowlairs	141,244	
31/7/58-29/8/58**NC(EO)** Cowlairs	26,488	26,488
17/11/58-2/12/58**LC(EO)** Cowlairs	37,717	37,717
29/12/59-10/1/59**LC** Cowlairs	39,947	353
17/1/59-9/3/59**HC(EO)** Cowlairs	40,263	669
6/5/59-11/5/59**NC** Cowlairs	48,443	8,849
16/6/59-11/7/59**LC** Cowlairs		
21/10/59-6/11/59**LC** Cowlairs		
16/11/59-25/12/59**LC** Cowlairs		
14/3/60-16/3/60**NC(EO)** Cowlairs		
15/7/60**NC(EO)** Cowlairs	98,984	24,890
22/7/60-17/9/60**HG** Cowlairs	100,620	26,526
29/9/60**NC(EO)** Cowlairs	342	26,868

BOILERS
833 from new
964 24/10/55
835 17/9/60

ANNUAL MILEAGE
1952 60,126
1953 64,296
1954 62,531
1955 53,805
1956 64,694
1957 52,879
1958 39,594
1959 34,500
1960 39,567

Condemned 4/12/65.
Stored Kingmoor 12/65-2/66, cut up Cambells, Airdrie 3/66.

Above. **72007 CLAN MACKINTOSH (the Clans, especially, acquired that 'foreign' look when viewed from this angle) at Carnforth shed in July 1964. The 'flexible screen' looks more sad and tired than ever by this late time. This picture shows well the sieve box slung under the tender tank and the discreet way the AWS cylinder is stowed under the left-hand side of the cab. Photograph D.H. Beecroft, The Transport Treasury.**

72008 CLAN MACLEOD

Date to traffic 14/3/52
Tender: BR1 No.792

SHEDS
Kingmoor 14/3/52

REPAIRS

9/6/54-4/8/54**LI** Crewe	153,467	29,655
R3622 alteration to spring balancing arrangement and fitting of stops to prevent reversing gear jamming		
R3242 alterations to pony truck lubricators		
R3400 manganese liners to intermediate rubbing plates and intermediate buffer faces		
3/1/55-26/2/55**LC** St Rollox	23,979	(1955) 2
13/10/56-24/11/56**HG** St Rollox	121,155	51,270
22/12/56-29/12/56**LC** St Rollox	4,255	55,525
15/1/57-28/2/57**NC(EO)** St Rollox	5,988	1,596
R5674 atomiser and bogie lubrication, R5764/5 eliminate steam dryer		
R5764 safety links		
R5777 "remove Downs sanding"		
R5772 leading axle protection shield R5900 Safety links between engine & tender		
9/11/57-16/11/57**LC(EO)** St Rollox	56,633	52,241
1/3/58-19/4/58**HI** Cowlairs	74,903	10,757
13/7/59-17/7/59**NC(EO)** Cowlairs		
23/12/59-13/2/60**LI** Cowlairs		
6/9/60-8/10/60**LC(EO)** Cowlairs	29,814	29,814
17/10/60-12/11/60**LC** Cowlairs	30,160	30,160

BOILERS
834 from new
831 24/11/56

ANNUAL MILEAGE
1952 60,806
1953 63,006
1954 53,632
1955 45,908
1956 55,662
1957 59,754
1958 52,336
1959 56,248
1960 35,156

Condemned 16/4/66.
Stored at Kingmoor 4-6/66, cut up McWilliams, Shettleston 6/66

72009 CLAN STEWART
Date to traffic 26/3/52
Tender: BR1 No.793

SHEDS
Kingmoor 26/3/52
Eastern Region 13/9/58
Kingmoor 25/10/58

REPAIRS

18/4/52-17/5/52**LC** Crewe	3,660	3,660
5/2/53-14/2/53**LC(EO)** St Rollox	57,936	5,872
BW1533 fitting draught excluders		
4/10/54-9/11/54**LI** Crewe	165,020	46,154
R3622 alteration to spring balancing arrangement and fitting of stops to prevent reversing gear jamming		
R3242 alterations to pony truck lubricators		
R3400 manganese liners to intermediate rubbing plates and intermediate buffer faces		
R3682 fitting new type drawhook rubbers		
R4194 new type drain plugs on Timken roller bearing axles		
6/9/55-20/10/55**HC(EO)** Crewe	56,345	49,178
16/11/55-2/12/55**LC(EO)**	56,932	49,765
14/1/57-1/3/57**HG** St Rollox	120,870	2,417
R3345 atomiser modification		
R5674/5 elimination of steam drier		
E2948 alteration frames and spring bracket		
R4906 new chimney rings		
R5900 safety links between engine & tender		
R6132 protection shield over axle		
19/7/58**HI** Cowlairs	75,218	21,115
23/11/59-30/12/59**LC(EO)** Cowlairs		
27/1/60-20/2/60**LC(EO)** Cowlairs	75,525	2,838
8/11/60-22/12/60**LI** Cowlairs	110,260	37,575
13/6/61-18/7/61**LC(EO)** Cowlairs	15,832	15,586
24/8/61-5/9/61**LC(EO)** Cowlairs	22,148	21,902

BOILERS
835 from new
834 1/3/57

ANNUAL MILEAGE
1952 52,064
1953 66,802
1954 53,321
1955 45,908
1956 57,241
1957 56,520
1958 43,848
1959 49,952
1960 37,821
Condemned 28/8/65.
Stored Kingmoor 8-11/65, cut up Motherwell Machinery and Scrap Co, Wishaw 12/65

HENGIST: THE 1000th STANDARD?

The HENGIST dream began early in 1993 when the original members, inspired by the A1 project, determined upon building a new steam locomotive. The 'Hengist 72010 Locomotive Group' was born, the decision to build a new Clan coming after much discussion as to which loco could be built, taking into account cost, availability of drawings, ease of construction and maintenance. That done, the group's first publicity shot came in December 1993 in *Railway World*. The same article appeared in 1994 editions of *Railway Magazine* and *Steam Classic* penned by our Chairman, Paul Burns. Much more publicity has come later through Irwell Press and *British Railways Illustrated* in particular. Enough support had been gained by 1995 for the AGM of that year to unanimously vote to change to a limited company and in April 1996 **The Standard Steam Locomotive Company Ltd** was formally registered at Companies House. In August the first part was made, a humble washer for engine-tender drawbar but it was a start. Becoming a registered charity was next and we gained this status in May 1997; not long after this the HENGIST nameplates were cast. The Swanage Railway kindly gave us a home at their Herston locomotive works in February 1999. Publicity remains the key to success and in February 2000 many magazines featured the now-famous 'cab in the bedroom' scene.

We now have all the pieces necessary to assemble the smokebox as a completed item and work continues on the cab; all the larger parts are now made and work can now start on the smaller ones. October 2000 saw the first BR Standard chimney to be cast for over forty years delivered to Herston Works.

In April 2000 our hundredth member signed on the dotted line. The rear extension frames were cut and machined by Jaymee Profiles of Wolverhampton and many more items have followed, including whistle valve, steam lance cock, firehole door forgings, cab handrail forgings, fishtail, square damper operating bar forgings, most waterfeed parts, bogie sideplay spring components and forgings and front tender steps. The squint glasses brass parts were ordered, the front tubeplate pressed and skimmed (machined around outside) and the snifting valves ordered.

It is agreed that 2002 will be 'The year of the Frames' and all fund-raising efforts will be directed to financing the purchase of these most important items. A BR Smiths Speedo was added to the collection in December, the horn guides for the frames arrived and membership is rising steadily above a hundred. The author has been a signed up member for several years.

Become one of HENGIST's growing band of followers; write to Russell Newland (Secretary), 84 Billet Road, Roselane Gate, Chadwell Heath, Essex, RM6 5PP. 0208 598 9468; russel.newland@linklaters.com Photograph The Transport Treasury.

Below. **The end came for 'the Polmadie five' at Darlington Works, curiously. They were withdrawn when BR was still scrapping its own; by the time the second five were withdrawn, in 1965-66, private scrap yards were being used. It is said that the first five were stripped for spares but it seems unlikely; perhaps if 'the cry went out' Darlington might have forwarded a spare part to Kingmoor but these two here look no more stripped than would be expected for their final journeys. Withdrawn at the end of 1962 72003 and 72002, at least, were still intact when this photograph was taken nearly a year later, on 6 November 1963.**